LOVE WORK

Creative Tactics for Motivating Employees, Improving Retention and Attracting the Best New Recruits

First published in Great Britain in 2014 by

Fresh Future Ltd

Unit 6B Wingbury Courtyard Business Village

Wingrave, Aylesbury, Buckinghamshire

HP22 4LW

Printed and bound in the UK.

British Library Cataloguing in Publication Data ISBN 978-0-9563621-6-2

TABLE OF CONTENTS

WHY YOU SHOULD READ THIS BOOK

Ask the leaders of the world's most successful companies what their greatest business asset is and they will almost certainly tell you it's their people. After all, it has been proven that businesses with a great work place culture achieve three times the return that the average business achieves.*

However, attracting and retaining employees who are committed to the success and sustainability of these businesses isn't something that happens by accident. Nor are the things that truly motivate and engage these workforces necessarily the ones that many employers would expect.

How to get the very best out of a workforce is a conundrum that has been faced by businesses since time immemorial, and, of course, the problem is made even more difficult by the fact that the motivational tactics and initiatives that might have been effective 10 or 20 years ago are likely to have little impact today.

However, despite the inescapable differences between generations of workers, today's employers often behave as though they're stuck in a time warp, trapped in the days before the internet became such an integral part of our everyday lives and when money was the only carrot worth dangling to attract and retain great employees.

Though perhaps worst of all, many of these companies are still under the illusion that the cream of the crop are happy just to be in a job... any job.

The result, not surprisingly, is that businesses which often have great potential are losing talented employees to companies which truly understand what makes the current generation tick and can offer a culture that both motivates and inspires them.

However motivating your existing employees and making your company the kind of business that the highest calibre workers want to join is far from beyond your reach... and it needn't cost you a fortune. Regardless of your position in your company, you will find many easily achievable ideas you can implement with your team.

In *Love Work*, we hope to give you an insight into what really matters for today's generation of workers by providing you with inspiration for improving the workplace and culture that you are responsible for, and helping your business to attract and retain the best. It is also our hope that when it comes to hiring key people in your organisation, you will be prompted to consider us as partners who not only care genuinely about innovation in the workplace, but who can also help you find the very best employees.

So let's get started!

* Great Place to Work Study 2013 (GreatPlaceToWork.com/our-approach/what-are-the-benefits-great-workplaces)

INTRODUCTION

Setting up, growing and sustaining a successful business enterprise is challenging, and the task isn't made any easier because the conditions under which businesses operate change over time. Coping successfully with ever changing economies, technologies and consumer trends requires businesses to constantly reassess their products, services, marketing and distribution. Alongside all of this, if businesses are going to become and remain successful, they also have to evolve with the changing values and priorities of their workers.

The attitudes of past generations of workers have been characterised by qualities such as duty, sacrifice and employer loyalty. Their expectations have typically focused on things like financial rewards, better job titles and 'a job for life'. Then along came Generation Y and suddenly everything was turned on its head. Instead of aspiring to that symbolic gold watch and wanting to work in an environment where they were guided by structure, rules and where feedback was unwelcome, this new breed of workers wanted:

- Fun
- Sociability and the chance to work with people who inspired them
- The opportunity to use their creativity
- More training and opportunities

- A series of goals to work towards so that they could see what they had achieved and then have the chance to move on to something new
- Lots of feedback
- Meaning and fulfillment

This new generation also made it very clear that they expected rewards, although not necessarily in the form of the higher salaries and bonuses that their predecessors demanded. Life, for those of Generation Y, isn't about worshipping the god of money. It's about achieving fulfilment in a much wider sense - and that's something that doesn't come with a 'traditional' price tag!

Of course there's no getting away from the fact that any worker who isn't being paid a reasonable wage and receiving basic benefits isn't going to be entirely satisfied with his lot. According to one study, once these basic requirements have been met, the kinds of things that employees really desire are:

- Free beverages
- A smartphone or tablet for their own personal use, and even...
- Free shoulder massages

Now, whilst this might seem like a rather odd assortment of requests, when you look a little more closely you can see that what they all have in common is that they contribute to the individual recipient's overall sense of fulfilment.

Effectively, employers who provide rewards such as these say to their employee's:

"I recognise and appreciate you as a human being with a wide range of needs, rather than just another cog in the machine."

This basic need to be recognised as a 'whole' person, as well as an individual with something unique to offer, is high on the list of priorities for today's workers and, I would argue, for every human being. In the workplace though, this isn't something that can simply be achieved by putting a little extra in employees' pay packets or offering them a higher salary. In fact, a recent survey conducted by employeesing firm *Accountemps* clearly indicated that recognition is far more highly valued than pay increases and that providing recognition is one of the greatest ways to motivate employees. So money is not the 'be-all-and-end-all' in fact, in many cases what inspires employees to give their very best is something that can be given for free!

Especially in tough economic times when most employers aren't in a position to award salary increases and bonuses, this should of course come as great news because the lack of financial reward needn't have too negative an impact on workers' levels of motivation to stay with their current employer. In fact, according to a study conducted by *Employee Hold'em*, a massive 92% of employees reported that they would stay in their current job for less money if they were able to achieve the things that were truly important to them, such as a good work/life balance and appropriate recognition for their efforts.

Another clear example of this point comes from career analyst Dan Pink who, in his book *Drive – The Surprising Truth About What Motivates Us*, reveals that for those people who are engaged in non-manual work, the larger the reward, the lower the performance! Essentially, if employees are paid sufficiently well, so the topic of money is off the table, then three things become far more important, namely:

- Autonomy – the opportunity to direct yourself and make decisions on the best way to get a job done
- Mastery – the opportunity to blend knowledge and skills in order to master a subject or achieve a goal
- Purpose – the desire to make the world a better place, or as Dan Pink himself describes it "*to put a ding in the universe*"

It's not hard to see how all three of these factors might appeal to Generation Y, and those who follow them, as they fulfil the desires to:

- Be creative and have free rein to achieve specific goals
- Develop their knowledge through training and put that knowledge into practice in ways that are fun and satisfying
- Feel as though their work is meaningful

So, where does a business start in terms of creating a culture that not only recognises, rewards and retains its employees, but also attracts the highest calibre candidates... and indeed why should it bother?

The horrible truth is that the cost to employers of replacing employees is high. Not only do new employees have to be recruited and trained, but of course it takes time for them to become fully effective in their new roles, and that time costs money. It's hardly surprising that companies typically find themselves shelling out anything from 30-50% of a worker's annual wage to replace them... and that's just for an entry-level worker. Replacing a professional is likely to cost in the region of 150% of the individual's yearly salary, and by the time you get to the executive level, you could be paying out a whopping 500%!

On top of the more obvious financial costs of high employees turnover though, employing a workforce which is demotivated and disengaged has a whole host of 'hidden', but equally damaging implications. Think of the price that organisations around the world must pay when undervalued and demoralised employees:

- Continually turn up late for work, or
- Don't turn up at all
- Imagine the impact on sales, not to mention business reputation, when:
- Customers and clients are faced with company representatives who are clearly dispirited and deflated, or

- Employees express their negativity outside of the workplace, either in face-to-face interactions or via social media websites

and how:

- Fraud
- Theft of company resources, and
- Workplace conflicts fuelled by employee dissatisfaction could impact on a business' bottom line.

Of course there are those employers who would be only too happy to lay the blame for their employeesing woes firmly at the feet of Generation Y and Millennial workers, who are often viewed as:

- Pampered and spoilt
- Over-confident to the point of cockiness
- Expecting everything to be handed to them on a plate, and
- Only interested in themselves

These new generations, however, are merely products of the world that they have grown up in; a 'dog eat dog' world of rampant technological progress in which everything can be had 'at the click of a mouse'. Far from responding with attitudes that might typify such an upbringing though, in fact most have rebelled and instead seek meaning in their lives and the opportunity to play a part in making the world a better place. In many respects, what they actually represent is a desire to return to the old-fashioned values of respect, inclusion and plain good manners, and who can blame them for expecting a simple 'Thank you' and a pat on the back for a job well done?

For today's employers who are not only faced with new generations of workers, but also older generations who are increasingly adopting similar priorities and values, the choice is quite simple. They can either adapt to these changed expectations and needs and create a company culture that motivates and inspires their employee's, or continue to treat them with fear and mistrust and effectively alienate them. To do the latter, however, is to court disaster.

What exactly do we mean by company culture though?

Probably one of the best ways to explain company culture is by describing it as a company's 'personality', but from an employee's perspective. Typically it is reflected in an organisation's mission and values, as well as in its business ethics, but it also speaks to the company's expectations and goals, its style of communication and its work environment. It describes, for example, whether a company operates in a more relaxed and informal style or whether it values teamwork, inclusion and openness to ideas.

Rather than being 'designed', company cultures develop naturally and evolve over time. William Rothwell, professor of education and workforce development at *Penn State's College of*

Education, made a very good point when he said that:

> *"the culture of an organisation is not just something you can announce with a slogan, but rather the end result of actions you've taken."*

As you can see then, every company without exception has a culture, elements of which might be dictated, for example, by the physical aspects of the workplace. A company which operates in an open-plan environment, therefore, is likely to develop a completely different culture to one which has individual offices. Other elements of company culture though, are typically passed down from the attitudes of the organisation's leaders. If those at the very top of the business make it clear that 'it's their way or the highway', for instance, then this attitude is likely to percolate through the entire company leaving employees feeling as though their ideas and suggestions are unwelcome.

The way that a business behaves, particularly towards its employees, sends out clear messages in terms of how those employees are perceived and whether or not they are valued. In turn, those messages will dictate whether your organisation is one that your existing employee's, not to mention those bright young individuals who are buoying your company up in terms of recruitment, want to be associated with. To quote from the *Hubspot* (an American tech business) Culture Code:

"Culture is to recruiting as product is to marketing. Customers are more easily attracted with a great product. Amazing people are more easily attracted with a great culture."

For existing employees, a great culture helps people to deliver their best work, but for potential candidates it can and does make the all-important difference between whether the very best people decide to join your organisation, or not. Gone are the days when job applicants just weighed up the salary and benefits when choosing which job offer to accept. Today they're also taking into account whether the culture of your business is one that would be a good fit for their aspirations. So, now is the time to change and improve how you incentivise, reward and develop the talent that's already in your business, as well as the talent that you hope to attract.

EMPLOYEE OF THE MONTH

PART 1
FRUGAL RECOGNITION

Most companies today offer different remuneration packages for different roles within their businesses. Sales employees, for instance, are often paid a flat-rate salary plus commission on the value of any sales or orders. This, of course, provides them with a great incentive to excel at their jobs and sell more.

In most other areas of the business, however, employees work for a salary which is fixed, irrespective of how well or how fast they carry out their tasks. However, turning in work ahead of a deadline or adding value to a task also benefits the company, but rarely are these occasions recognised, let alone rewarded by employers.

In some cases, the reason for going that extra mile might be an entirely personal one, such as if a worker is pursuing promotion or simply has a desire to satisfy his or her own sense of personal pride. Regardless of the stimulus behind it, however, there is still a benefit to the business and, if no appreciation is shown for the extra effort, the employee is very likely to exhaust their sense of motivation and then everyone loses out.

The benefits to a business when a salesperson lands a huge new contract or makes a massive sale are much more obvious than those gained in other ways, but that doesn't make them any less valuable. Make a point of noticing when employees who are on fixed salaries go that extra mile and use these occasions as an opportunity to say "Thank you" and offer a small reward.

The 'frugal treats' suggested here might cost your business little or nothing but they won't go unnoticed. If you want them to have maximum impact though, don't use them too regularly or let them become an expectation rather than a reward.

1. PUBLIC PRAISE

Everyone likes to be praised, but more than that they like to be praised in public. Why not use an occasion when a employees member has produced exceptional work or put in extra effort to write them an unprompted testimonial on their LinkedIn profile?

Giving praise on LinkedIn costs nothing more than a few minutes of your time but the effect gives the recipient valuable credibility as an employee. To make it particularly effective, be sure to be specific and reference the aspect of the individual's work that prompted you to write the testimonial. Alternatively, you could endorse them for a particular skill.

Oh, and don't worry that by praising your employee's publicly in this way they're going to be enticed away from your business by your competitors. It's recognition such as this that keeps employees loyal!

2. THE GIFT OF TIME

Who doesn't love to find themselves with an extra hour added on to their weekend, especially if it's unexpected?

Rewarding an employee by sending them home an hour early on a Friday does, of course, have a cost to the business. If one of your employees has managed to shave days or even weeks off a deadline though, or turned around an angry customer who might otherwise have gone elsewhere, an hour's salary is a small price to pay.

Another thing to remember is that because additional time off is something that's valued by most workers, and seeing a colleague leave that little bit early at the end of the week can be a great motivator for others.

3. THE PRIME SPOT

For many workers, just finding any parking spot is a relief after driving round in circles for what feels like hours in the morning. Imagine then, how delighted a deserving employee might feel to be allocated a priority parking spot at the office as a reward for doing a great job?

Priority parking spots are a bit like executive chairs – they somehow manage to make everyone who uses them feel special and just a tiny bit powerful. So, why not designate the best spot (typically the one closest to the office door!) specifically for the purpose of making great workers feel like the MD for the day!

4. THERE IS SUCH A THING

There's only one thing better than a meal you didn't cook yourself, and that's one you didn't pay for yourself!

Lunch on the company is both an effective and inexpensive way to say "Thanks" for a job well done, but this idea works even better for rewarding a great team effort because it feels more like a celebration.

You can either stump up for a meal in the employee canteen or restaurant if your company provides one, or get a general consensus on the type of food the team enjoys and order something in.

5. HEALTHY BOOST

Another great way to reward a team or department that's risen to the occasion and pulled out all the stops when it was needed, is to buy them a hamper filled with a selection of tasty fruits so that there's something for everyone to enjoy.

While fruit hampers work well as a one-off treat for a specific sector of an organisation that has exceeded expectations, if you want to achieve a more lasting effect on your workforce, then why not consider a regular weekly fruit delivery for everyone?

With sickness and ill health costing industry billions every year, obviously the health and well-being of employees should be high on the list of an employer's priorities. Providing a constant supply of nutritious snacks for them to munch on, especially mid-afternoon when energy levels typically start to flag, will make it far less likely that they'll seek out their daily 'fix' from the chocolate machine. The vegetable box company *Riverford.co.uk* actually sell a 'fruit box for work' which makes this easy to achieve.

Of course, not everyone is a huge fan of fresh fruit, so if you think a fruit hamper might not hit the spot, then another great alternative which offers good value for money are the graze boxes available through graze.com. For just a few pounds each, including delivery, your boxes are delivered direct to the workplace via Royal Mail and come filled with a whole range of tasty treats such as nuts, dried fruits, dips and dippers, delicious seeds and even some of the healthier sweet treats like flapjacks and popping corn.

As well as being a very cost-effective option for businesses, providing healthy snacks on a regular basis sends out the message to workforces that their employers care about their well-being, and it's the type of gesture that employees tend to mention when talking about their work environment with others. Imagine – all that great press from a humble fruit hamper!

6. FAMILY CONTRIBUTION

Sadly, recognising employees as human beings rather than just payroll numbers doesn't always come naturally to some businesses. All of the people who make up your workforce though, not only have whole other lives outside the company, but families and friends too. These people often do a great deal to support your workers in everything from covering the household chores while they're away on company business to helping them to stay motivated when times get tough or stressful. In supporting your employee's, of course, they are in turn supporting your business, so why not use the festive season as an opportunity to thank them personally for their contributions?

Not surprisingly, a corporate Christmas card with an anonymous squiggle at the bottom isn't going to convey the right message, so make sure that you enclose a personal note which thanks the individual's partner for his or her support. Both the card and the note should be hand-written and signed by hand and, for maximum effect, be sure to post the envelope to the recipient's home address rather than getting your employee to deliver it on your behalf.

Of course, you don't have to wait until Christmas to express your thanks and appreciation to the families of your employees. Any event or occasion which has led to partners being called upon to provide higher levels of support, such as through a stressful company reorganisation or when they've been working hard to secure a big new contract, can represent another opportunity to say a personal 'Thank you'.

Do remember when making gestures of this sort, that it's not about looking as though you care, but about truly caring. Behind every one of your employee's there are people who make it possible for them to deliver their best to your organisation, so take the time to really appreciate the daily support they offer.

7. COMPANY STUDIO

What better advert for your company, and what better way to show your great company culture than fun and funky photos of your employees taken in the workplace?

Many people struggle to find suitable photographs of themselves for *LinkedIn,* and *Twitter* profiles that don't make them look as though they've taken part in a police line-up. By hiring a professional photographer to visit your office, you can not only provide your workers with some great material but demonstrate your company's sense of fun, innovation and creativity at the same time.

8. RETAIL CLUBS

All of the rewards and incentives that we've looked at so far represent excellent, low-cost ways to show employees that their efforts are recognised and valued. Particularly in the case of employees on fixed salaries though, nothing is appreciated quite as much as a gesture which essentially puts more money in their pockets.

Whilst there's a whole raft of different schemes that allow employers to provide benefits to their workers, such as free shopping vouchers through *Flexbank*, many of these require a fair degree of financial and organisational commitment to get them off the ground and maintain them. One really simple way to give employees more spending power though, is by buying your workers membership cards for local bulk retailers such as *Costco*.

Membership warehouses such as these typically carry quality, brand name merchandise at considerably lower prices than other retailers, giving employee's access to discounts on everyday essentials. Making their money go further gives employees extra funds for holidays and luxury items; and guess who they're going to be thinking about, and thanking, every time they use that card!

PART 2
SHOW APPRECIATION FOR THE TRAVELLERS

Not only has the globalisation of business markets brought about dramatic changes in the way that companies conduct their day-to-day affairs, but it has also had a considerable impact on the working lives of a great many individual employees. National and international contracts with suppliers and customers (both current and potential) necessitate levels of business travel that would have been unheard of even a couple of decades ago.

Although many employers seem to view business trips as perks of the job, for the individuals who have to undertake them they typically present a number of challenges, such as:

- Being away from family and loved ones
- Loneliness
- The cold anonymity of hotel rooms
- Tiring and sometimes stressful journeys
- No 'recovery' time between the trip itself and being back in the workplace

- Unfamiliar surroundings, language and cultural issues and 'strange' food
- No 'down-time' whilst travelling

In addition, there are usually dozens of arrangements to be made and numerous personal and professional bases to cover before they even set out, including:

- Making travel arrangements – many employees don't have PAs or secretaries to do this on their behalf
- Finding cover for their normal workplace responsibilities
- Making personal arrangements, to ensure that family members, children, pets and even the garden are all taken care of during their absence
- Washing, ironing and packing

All of these essential tasks soon start to eat into workers' leisure time, as does the travelling itself, but rarely are they compensated for this, either in financial terms or through time off in lieu.

During times of economic difficulty, especially, most employers restrict business travel so that only the most important or urgent journeys are undertaken. When employees do go away, therefore, it tends to be in connection with critical business matters where the employer would certainly want their representative to arrive feeling fresh, relaxed and on top of their game.

The tips that follow, offer a number of low-cost suggestions to help take some of the pain out of travelling long distances for business purposes, as well as reducing the chores that your employees typically have to face on their return.

9. AIRPORT HASSLE

No journey, whether it's for the purposes of business or pleasure, starts the minute the plane takes off or when the train leaves the station, and, often, the most stressful part is getting from home to the next point of departure on time. So, rather than leaving employees to face that initial drive, why not pay for a taxi to pick them up from home and let someone else take the strain?

Alternatively, for those who prefer to make their own way to the airport, you could allow them to use car parks that have a pick-up and drop-off service. As well as sparing them the mad dash from the long-stay car park to the terminal at the start of the journey, the time saving at the end of a long week when they're tired and desperate to get home will be a godsend.

10. EXECUTIVE LOUNGE

Airport terminals typically aren't the most relaxing or comfortable places to kill time when you're waiting to check-in or board a plane, especially when there are flight delays and cancellations. Hard metal seats that seem to be designed specifically to discourage passengers from sitting still for too long, noise and crowds can all conspire to make stress levels soar, not to mention making it impossible to use the time constructively by finalising work preparations. Even on long haul trips though, many businesses simply can't afford to fly their employees Business Class, but that doesn't mean that the airport experience needs to be a miserable one.

With three different plans available for occasional, more frequent and regular travellers, *Priority Pass* (prioritypass.com) offers a great membership scheme which allows access to high quality VIP lounges at around 600 airports in more than 100 countries around the world. Members don't need to pre-book, but can simply turn up at any of the lounges and make use of the facilities whenever they choose, irrespective of which airline they are travelling with or which class they're flying. There's even a 'Lounge Finder' mobile app which can be downloaded for free and where travellers can find details of what's available where.

Membership provides access to comfortable areas away from the hustle and bustle of the main airport terminal, as well as free refreshments and snacks and complimentary newspapers and magazines. Whether they want to catch up on the day's news on television or access e-mail and the internet, your employees will be guaranteed a quieter spot away from the chaos where they're less likely to have other travellers looking over their shoulders. Some VIP lounges even provide showers, games rooms and cinemas for their guests and, for an additional cost, bedrooms, massages and beauty treatments.

At a cost of just over £200 for annual membership of the highest level Prestige plan, your business could truly make a difference in terms of ensuring that your frequent flyers arrive at their destinations feeling calm and relaxed. More than that though, this small commitment to their comfort is certain to demonstrate that you value and appreciate the additional time and effort they've had to expend to travel on your company's behalf.

11. AIRPLANE UPGRADE

Recognising employees who go the extra mile for your company often doesn't require grand or expensive gestures, and typically it's the little things that demonstrate thought and consideration. In the case of those whose roles involve frequent business travel, just knowing that someone in their organisation has acknowledged that their journeys are often tiring and stressful is something in itself, and even a relatively low-cost solution to improving their situation is greatly appreciated.

We've all found ourselves seated close to a crying baby, a bored youngster or a chatty adult in the tight confines of an aeroplane at some time, and even when we've been travelling for pleasure, most of us will have experienced the frustration of not being able to sleep or concentrate on reading a book or doing a crossword. While such occasions can be annoying, of course it's not so bad when you know that you can relax when you get to your destination. For business travellers who often don't have the luxury of any recovery time though, and who often need to spend their journeys preparing for important meetings, these kinds of distractions and interruptions can make for an exhausting flight.

Although you could choose to spend more, just £50 is enough to buy a highly effective pair of noise-cancelling headphones to provide a bit of much-needed peace and quiet for your frequent flyers or those on long haul trips. These help to block out both the noise of the other passengers and the sound of the aircraft engines, which many people find exhausting in itself, allowing your employees to arrive feeling more relaxed and refreshed.

12. HOME HELP

As we mentioned at the start of this chapter, business travel doesn't just involve additional work and stress during the journey itself, but also before your employees even set off and following their return. One great way to show your appreciation, therefore, is by taking some of the grind out of their home life as soon as they get back.

One of the biggest nightmares whenever we get back from a spell away from home is the huge suitcase of laundry, and of course for business travellers who usually need to get straight back into the workplace, making sure that this is washed and ironed is an immediate priority. Employing a local service to launder, or even just to iron your employees' clothes on their return, however, allows them more time to relax and recover from their journey.

Time doesn't just stand still while your workers are away on business. The grass continues growing and the dust keeps on settling on the furniture. Why not book them a cleaner or arrange for someone to cut the lawn and tidy up the garden when they get back? Website company *Weebly* give all employees a $50 monthly credit towards housekeeping regardless of whether that person is travelling.

Remember that even if your employee doesn't live alone, these chores are ones that he or she would almost certainly take some responsibility for if they were at home to do so. Don't just expect their loved ones to take up the slack in their absence, but instead provide some extra help so that the whole family can spend some quality time together.

CLIMBING TRIP

PART 3
BIGGER REWARDS

The reward and recognition schemes that we have looked at so far have all been low-cost options which are ideal for businesses of any size, as well as for those which have been hit hard by the recent recession. Not all of today's companies are struggling in the current economic crisis, and in many cases the reason they have managed to escape the worst is as a direct result of the commitment and loyalty shown by their employee's. In these cases, employers may well be in a position to offer larger or longer-term rewards to ensure that their workers remain engaged.

Even in smaller businesses or those which are still going through tough times, the cost of offering the occasional big reward for exceptional performance can be more than offset by the impact on employee engagement and the resulting increases in productivity and employee retention.

13. PEER RECOGNITION

Although many businesses operate bonus schemes, typically these involve managers nominating worthy employees for additional rewards. Now, while there is some merit in any scheme that recognises exceptional performance, scaling up a system which is inherently limited by the ratio of managers to workers can often prove impossible. A peer-to-peer bonus system, on the other hand, allows the recognition of more of your employees, at the same time as promoting better employee relations.

As the name suggests, a peer-to-peer bonus system is one which gives every employee the opportunity to award a bonus to a colleague who they feel has gone beyond the call of duty or achieved something exceptional, with the only proviso being that the colleague must be at the same level as themselves or in a more junior position. The bonus could be a straightforward cash reward or it could offer a cash equivalent. Alternatively, you could run a system similar to that adopted by US-based online retailer *Zappos*, which allows its workers to award either cash or 'Zollars' – the company's own currency which can be redeemed against their own-brand products, cinema tickets or items sold through their internal 'Zollar store'. If they prefer, recipients can even convert their 'Zollars' into cash and donate it to charity.

Being recognised and rewarded by management is important to most employees, but knowing they have the respect and appreciation of the colleagues with whom they work and interact on a daily basis, and being rewarded for this, is in many ways even more valuable to employees.

14. MAKE 'EMPLOYEE OF THE YEAR' MEAN SOMETHING BIG

Especially in larger organisations where there are greater numbers of employees and therefore more competition for the title, winning the 'Employee of the Year' Award really ought to be a big deal. According to research though, the very employees who stand to be nominated for the award actually place little or no importance on this annual event. Why? Because often it turns out to be a bit of a 'non-event' involving a brief ceremony held at the employee's own workplace and during which no-one (often including the recipient of the award!) really learns why it was awarded.

If 'Employee of the Year' is going to be in any way meaningful in terms of recognising, rewarding and motivating employees, then it needs to make the winner feel like a superstar. Don't just make sure that all of your other employee's know who won, but publicise the winner's name and photograph to your customers and suppliers too.

Another great way to maximise the sense of kudos that the winner experiences is by having 'Employee of the Year 2014' printed on their business cards. Once earned, of course, this title should remain on their cards in years to come, so that everyone the individual comes into contact with knows that they are dealing with a representative that the company itself has recognised for his or her outstanding performance.

Here are some other ways to shout out the individual's success from the rooftops:

- Put an award notice with the winner's photograph on a main noticeboard so that employees and visitors alike can see it when they enter the building. Better still, have a gallery of current and past award winners on display.
- Allow the winner to include 'Employee of the Year 2014' at the bottom of all their internal memos and in their e-mail footers
- Highlight the winner's success in a testimonial on their LinkedIn profile
- Make space on the agenda at company update meetings to publicise the award winner and the reasons for his or her success
- Attach one of the winner's specially-printed business cards to a greetings card and send it to their spouse, their partner or even their parents with a message to thank them for supporting your employee whilst he or she worked so hard throughout the year

Important Tip!

There are a few suggestions throughout this book that involve sending different kinds of 'Thank You' notes or cards, but as with all good stuff in life, the devil is in the detail. Always make sure that your messages, as well as the envelopes they're being sent in, are hand-written, and always use a proper stamp rather than running them through the franking machine. Also, if you want your gesture to have maximum impact, never use your employee as a courier. Instead, address the envelope to the recipient's home address and send it through the mail.

15. CHEEKY WEEKENDS

As we've mentioned previously, it isn't just your employees who feel the effects of your business' particularly busy times. Spouses and partners feel them too, and often it is their support which is key in ensuring that your employee's are able to deliver such great results.

Rather than just sending a note or a card to express your appreciation to an employee's nearest and dearest, consider rewarding them both with a well-deserved weekend away together. Send the money directly to the individual's partner with an personal letter of thanks so that he or she feels properly recognised, as well as gaining maximum impact in terms of the surprise factor.

16. BONUS LEAVE

One of the really important aspects of employee recognition and reward schemes lies in acknowledging that not all of your employees are the same. What appeals to one might be another's worst nightmare. Since holidays and the opportunity to travel are valued highly by some workers though, giving employees the chance to buy additional annual leave can be a huge factor in terms of engendering company loyalty and improving levels of employee engagement.

In order to protect your own business interests, you will of course want to put certain restrictions in place when offering a benefit such as this. Make it a proviso that the option to purchase additional leave does not apply:

- During the first year of employment
- To anyone who is still fulfilling a period of probation
- To anyone whose performance is under review

17. CULTURAL EXPERIENCES

When most employers think about developing their employee's, generally what they have in mind is sending them on a few role-related training courses or, at best, a team-building event. Developing employees in a wider sense, however, can deliver enormous business benefits at the same time as providing individual employees with life-changing experiences.

More so than ever before, today's businesses are working hand-in-hand with suppliers and customers who are not just based in different countries, but entirely different continents. Not surprisingly, the interactions with these foreign partners can sometimes be fraught with misunderstandings arising from both language and cultural differences. Offering employees an incentive which encourages them to broaden their horizons through international travel can serve a dual purpose for the business. Gaining greater cultural awareness creates a well rounded and knowledgeable workforce that becomes much more confident operating in international markets.

For employees who are considering visits to far-flung places such as South America, New Zealand or China, you could, for example, offer some additional days' holiday and a financial contribution towards their trip to actively encourage them to venture further afield. Of course, you're going to want to make sure that all your employee's don't disappear at once, so you could either limit your incentive to a certain number of employees each year or only make it available, say once every three years, for each employee.

18. LUGGAGE PARTY

One of the criticisms that's sometimes levelled at employers in relation to employee recognition and reward schemes is that they're not entirely 'inclusive' because they're limited, for example, to those in sales-related roles. One great way to overcome this and ensure that all employees have the opportunity to benefit from the organisation's appreciation, as well as to generate a sense of excitement, is to follow the example of US law firm *Freeborn & Peters* by throwing a luggage party.

The way it works is that on a pre-arranged Friday, all employees bring a packed suitcase with them to the office. Four names are then drawn from a hat and those individuals are then whisked away on an all-expenses-paid luxury trip. In the case of *Freeborn & Peters*, the lucky winners head off for four glorious days in Las Vegas, but of course your chosen location could be anywhere that's both exciting and appealing to the majority of your workers.

19. HOLIDAY PROPERTY

Investing in a holiday property for use by employees isn't something that all businesses can afford, but for those looking to make an investment, providing somewhere that employees can take off to at short notice and at minimal or no cost to themselves, can represent a rare and valuable incentive in terms of attracting and retaining employees.

One UK company which has embraced this particular tactic is the department store, *John Lewis PLC*. The company currently owns five different properties which are put at the disposal of its employees, including a castle, a country house and even a water sports club.

When choosing an appropriate property for use by your employee's, the key is to focus on those which are a manageable journey away from where your employee's are based so that they can easily escape for a weekend. As well as ensuring comfortable facilities and offering an environment where there's a variety of activities, the property should also have a dedicated work area so that they can visit with their families during the week, have somewhere to work if needed and yet still be able to switch off and relax. A nearby beach resort can often make an ideal choice, but if your employees are based further inland, then why not consider a water sports centre, or even a ski resort?

If you want to cover some of the costs of maintaining and cleaning the property, there is the option to charge employees a nominal amount for its use, or alternatively you could make staying there completely free of charge. Either way, the chances are that the property itself will appreciate in value, making it a great investment for your business. In the meantime, of course, your existing employees will have far more opportunities to relax, unwind and return to work feeling refreshed, and your business is likely to be way ahead of the competition when it comes to attracting great new employees. After all, how many companies do you know of that can boast a holiday property as a company perk?

20. EVENING CLASSES

As we mentioned earlier, employee development in most companies tends to be restricted to on and off-the-job training which is directly related to job role and normally takes place in company time. While some organisations are prepared to fund or subsidise education outside the workplace, even then they will often only stump up the cash if there is a direct link between the subject of the course and the individual's day-to-day tasks and responsibilities and if they can see a direct benefit to their own businesses.

The thing about any education or training course though, is that whilst it might focus on teaching a particular subject or practising a specific skill, in every case it actually requires the student to draw on a much wider variety of traits and develop a diverse range of abilities. Even if a course appears to bear no relation to the student's immediate job role, many of the competencies that he or she would need to use in the course of learning something new are ones which are highly valuable and sought-after in the workplace.

Let's take, for example, a sales manager who wants to do a course in creative writing. What possible benefits could you, the employer, derive from funding his or her education? Here are just a few ideas:

- Improved time management skills - combining a course of study with work, family responsibilities, running a home and fitting in a social life requires the development of superb time management skills which, once learned, can equally be applied in the workplace
- The improvement of basic language skills – this could result, for example, in the production of better quality sales proposals or lead to specialisation in the writing of bid responses
- Development of creativity – the creative muscle is much like any physical muscle in the body - if you don't use it, you lose it. Creative writing gets people into the habit of constantly generating new ideas, a skill which could be applied to coming up with proposals for great new products and services or innovative ways of selling.

- Development of problem-solving abilities – building plots and trying to find ways of getting characters into or out of situations in ways that seem plausible might not appear to have much in connection with solving problems in the workplace. Actually though, both require imagination, logic and reasoning.

Add to this, patience, determination, tenacity and a whole host of other skills and traits and suddenly that creative writing course isn't looking quite so irrelevant after all. In fact, if you look at just about any educational course, you're certain to find that the same is true.

Helping employees to further their education in whatever direction they choose is also a great way for managers to identify talents that might otherwise have been undiscovered, and even to redeploy workers to different areas of the business where they could become an even greater asset. Put another way, it can help businesses to fit round pegs into round holes.

21. BOOK WORMS

If funding or subsidising adult education doesn't seem like a viable option for your business, then why not take a leaf out of business communication technology company *Twilio's* book and buy each of your employees a *Kindle*, as well as providing them with a monthly allowance to spend on the book downloads of their choice?

Books, like travel and educational courses, broaden the mind and open up the imagination, irrespective of whether they're fiction or non-fiction, biographies or blockbusters. So, give your workers free access to whatever reading material appeals to them personally and watch them take off on their own little adventures of the mind.

Most people are open to educating themselves, especially in ways that feel fun and enjoyable, and really it's just about making it easy for them to do just that.

22. TRAIN FOR THE FUTURE

Many of the bright, well-educated new recruits who are entering the workplace nowadays are having to accept junior or entry-level positions just to get a foot in the door. In many cases these talented individuals are very capable of learning quickly and moving up the ladder, but unless employers can offer them the opportunity to develop their skills and knowledge, and can show them a clear path of progression, they're unlikely to stick around. By funding additional training for those who have proven themselves or done something to stand out in positive ways, companies can not only hang on to their best new employees, but also factor them into their succession plans.

In their bids to demonstrate their willingness to develop their employee's, many companies make the mistake of signing their employees up to learn skills that the business really has little or no need for. Far from motivating their workers, however, this actually just causes them intense frustration and often results in them moving on to pastures new so that they can put their new skills and knowledge into practice. When funding additional training, therefore, it's important to ensure that the skills and competencies acquired are relevant to the business and that they will lead directly to the individual becoming, for example, the next Department Supervisor or Manager.

Today's generation of workers needs a direct line of sight to the next rung of the professional ladder, so reward your best new workers with the opportunities to move them ever closer to their goals and not only will your business be rewarded with greater employee loyalty, but you'll be creating your next tranche of managers who will be ready to step in as positions become vacant.

23. REWARD FANS AND SUPPORTERS

Because the best employee reward and recognition schemes focus on making employees' lives as a whole easier or more enjoyable, another great treat that your business might like to offer is gift cards for gigs, comedy or sports events.

Supporting their favourite team or seeing their favourite band live is something that many people like to do in their spare time, although often their opportunities to do so are limited because of the cost. Providing gift cards for events such as these, therefore, really does feel like a special treat to most workers. Because it's totally unrelated to work or their professional or personal development, this also means that employees can accept the reward in the sure knowledge that there is no ulterior motive behind it.

Although there are greater costs associated with the rewards and incentives that we have covered in this chapter, it's well worth remembering that your company can derive lots of really positive PR from them by mentioning them in everything from company newsletters to social media sites. Also, even companies which do offer bigger rewards lose the odd employee but their rates of employee turnover are considerably lower and not only do their employees stay for longer, but they're far more productive during the time they're with the organisation!

BUSINESS CARD

PART 4
DEVELOPING A HABIT OF APPRECIATION

In many organisations, employee reward and incentive schemes are directly related to how well the company is doing. If sales are up, employees are rewarded, either with a financial bonus or some type of benefit in kind. In many cases though, the amount of effort that's put in and the dedication that's shown by workforces isn't necessarily reflected in higher revenue. A tough economic climate, for example, might make it virtually impossible to maintain or increase previous levels of sales however hard employees work. Nevertheless, the need still exists to ensure that workers stay motivated and feel valued by their employers, otherwise great people will be lost to the competition.

In this chapter, we're going to look at a few ideas for showing appreciation and keeping employees morale high, some of which even have the added benefit of helping to boost company sales and improve business reputation.

24. SURPRISE THEM

Who doesn't love the chance to leave work early, especially if that opportunity comes along unexpectedly?

Seemingly impromptu employee activity days are an excellent way to treat and reward your workforce, precisely because of the surprise factor. There's almost something 'naughty' about downing tools in the middle of the day after expecting to put in a full day, and it's that feeling of playing truant that typically makes the event all the more enjoyable.

Of course, one of the real keys to making employee activity days work is by ensuring that they take place entirely in company time. After all, who wants to work for an employer who forces them to come in on their own time... for any reason? So, every now and again, just close the office around midday and take everyone out for lunch, followed by some kind of fun activity. You might, for example:

- Book a private cinema, take your team to see the latest blockbusting film and throw in the drinks and popcorn as an additional treat

- Rent out a bowling alley, a skating rink, a go-kart track or a laser quest centre for a private event
- Organise a company picnic
- Arrange some exciting lessons to give your team the chance to try something new. How about taking them to a cookery school, organising archery lessons or lessons on how to play or a 'learn to play the drums
- Rent a box or book a private seating area and take your employees to see a local sports team play. Whether you choose a local football, rugby, cricket or ice hockey team though, do make sure that they're a decent one. After all, no-one other than a die-hard fan wants to sit and watch the local lads getting thrashed!
- Organise a trip to a local zoo or safari park or arrange for employees to be junior zoo keepers for the day or experience the world of falconry for some real hands-on fun
- Book a fabulous murder mystery afternoon at a local stately home or country house

Although surprise is key to making activity days a success, they do of course require planning, not to mention consideration for the different types of individual who are going to be taking part. Here are just some of the things to bear in mind when organising your event to make sure that it goes with a bang:

- Avoid activities that might make some people feel uncomfortable. Pushing Clive from I.T into taking part in bungee jumping might be more like a punishment than a treat and it certainly won't help with the bonding or friendship building process.

- Always make sure that there is no cost whatsoever to your employees, either in terms of money or their own free time
- Try not to make sweeping judgements in terms of what everyone will enjoy. Remember that not all of your employee's are likely to be extroverts who are up for anything, so try to avoid activities such as karaoke parties that put individuals directly in the spotlight.

25. SHARE THE SPOILS

Your employee's are the ones who are effectively working at the coal face, and if anyone's going to spot examples of waste or inefficiency in your business it's more likely to be them than 'the people upstairs'. Many will also have great ideas about how things could be done better, cheaper or quicker, but unless you give them an incentive to share their observations and ideas, they're simply going to go to waste.

Many organisations implement formal suggestion schemes aimed at collecting, recording and developing ideas from employees. Although these schemes often lead to reward and recognition sometimes the process prevents the development of a culture open to innovation . Worse still it can lead to a lack of willingness to adopt changes and new initiatives. The fact is that employees often come up with great suggestions 'off the cuff' and during the course of their normal working days, such as:

- Ideas for improving processes
- Ideas that improve the tools, materials and resources that they use in the course of their day-to-day work
- Ideas that improve products or margins
- Ideas that reduce operating costs or cut down on waste

Make the process of capturing and taking forward these ideas too cumbersome and, quite frankly, most employees just won't bother. Create a culture where employees feel free to voice their ideas in a less formal way, confident that managers will listen and in the knowledge that they stand to be recognised and rewarded, and everyone wins.

If it seems at all unlikely that your employees are going to come up with ideas that could make any significant impact on business performance or profitability, then just think about the worker at the MINI factory who came up with the inspired suggestion of recycling their cardboard packaging waste and using it for roof insulation in their vehicles. Not only did this cut out the need to buy-in the insulation, it also reduced their waste costs too. Now, there's a bit of out-of-the-box thinking that was worth a reward!

26. AMBASSADORS

Even most small businesses have their own dedicated sales employees, but any organisation operating in today's competitive marketplace which relies solely on these individuals is missing a trick.

Your company is probably made up of a variety of people in numerous different roles and, given the right culture, every single one of these individuals has the potential to be an ambassador for your business and to bring in new clients. People who are genuinely proud of the organisations they work for and who feel valued by their employers are, in many ways, the very best sales people. Not only are they keen to tell the world about the great products or services their company sells, but they're also often great at spotting potential new clients and markets.

Whilst it's often not advisable to let non-sales employees actually do the job of selling, giving them an incentive for suggesting new clients or coming up with ideas of possible joint ventures can mean identifying markets that may not even have been considered and open up some truly profitable doors. If you make your incentive contingent upon new leads actually becoming clients or joint venture partners then your business will have nothing to lose, but everything to gain.

27. A SENSE OF ACHIEVEMENT

Having said that, all of your employee's are potential ambassadors for your company, naturally it follows that you need to make it easy for every one of your employee's to promote what your company has to offer. What does that have to do with employee reward and recognition? Well, just think about the sense of excitement and personal pride that you experienced when you were given your first set of business cards.

Whilst they might cost next to nothing to produce, business cards typically have a huge impact on employees who wouldn't normally be issued with them, not least because they make employees such as general office workers and production staff feel trusted as representatives of their company. Providing them with a set of cards that bear their names and job titles sends a clear message that, in your organisation, you don't have to be part of the senior management team to be considered important... and that's one powerful message!

Of course, whatever size of business you represent, you're going to want to keep the costs of producing business cards down to a minimum. A great way to do this is to find a printer who can set you up with an online template, which means that each individual's cards can be created online and the normal artwork and proof costs can be saved. Often, this can mean a saving of more than 50% on what other printers might charge.

Another thing to consider is making it part of the deal with your chosen printing company that they supply each employee's business cards with a professional card holder. Not only will the holder avoid your employee's handing over creased and grubby business cards which are likely to reflect badly on your business, but they'll also add to the sense of pleasure and importance when you present them to your employees.

28. POSITIVE TESTIMONIALS

Whether for individual buyers looking to purchase something new, company representatives looking for new suppliers, businesses seeking out joint venture opportunities or jobseekers on the lookout for that perfect new role, the internet will almost certainly be their first stop when it comes to doing research. While online customer reviews and testimonials can help in terms of providing a glowing reference for your business, people often feel slightly dubious as to whether these are genuine. A positive testimonial for your company written by an employee, on the other hand, tends to have far greater impact.

The difference, of course, is one of perspective. A customer or client typically only has a limited interaction with the business that they're buying from, and whatever opinion they form of the company can only be that of an 'outsider'. An employee, however, has a much broader, 'inside' view. Even though the positive testimonial that he or she posts online might only focus on a particular aspect of the business, the reader tends to interpret the message as 'This is a great company overall'. After all, if a member of the workforce is prepared to put their own time and effort into praising their employer, they can't be a bad organisation to do business with.

Take a look at online jobs and careers community *Glassdoor* (glassdoor.com), whose content is generated entirely by employees, to get a feel for how powerful employee testimonials can be. Then, make it a practice to thank and reward your employee's for saying great things about the company.

29. EMPLOYEE SHARES

Employees who hold themselves fully accountable and have an 'owner's mentality' are the greatest assets to employers, so what better way to encourage them to think and behave like an owner than by giving them an opportunity to invest in your business?

Employee shares programmes represent a risk-free opportunity for workers to hold a stake in the companies they work for. Basically, workers pay into the scheme over an agreed term (typically three or five years) and if the company's share price goes up during that time, then workers can buy shares at the lower price fixed at the start of the programme term and sell them on for the higher price. If share prices fall, on the other hand, they get their money back along with a reasonable tax-free bonus. Now there's an incentive for your employees to work hard and make your business a success!

30. CLIENT SHARES

It might sound harsh, but many workers see their jobs as being about getting one project finished so that they can move on to the next. Naturally they want the client to be happy with the work they've produced, and somewhere in the backs of their minds they're probably vaguely aware that the sustainability and profitability of their own employer is dependent upon the sustainability and profitability of their client's business. On a day-to-day basis there's actually a disconnect between the fortunes of the two.

A great scheme used by New York advertising agency *Kirshenbaum Bond Senecal & Partners* not only helps to bridge the 'divide' between their own workers and the businesses of their clients, encouraging their employee's to take an active interest in the fortunes of their customers, but also rewards employees when these companies prosper.

The ad agency buys shares in its clients' businesses and then displays these companies' stock prices on a digital display board where they are prominently on view for all of their own employee's to see. This has the effect of encouraging their employees to think of their efforts as a direct contribution to boosting the shareholder value of their clients. And the reward? *Kirshenbaum Bond Senecal & Partners* sells the client stocks periodically and shares any dividend amongst its employees. Now there's a great incentive for a workforce to simultaneously look after its clients' interests and help improve its own company's reputation and profitability into the bargain!

FAMILY WEEK

PART 5
WORKPLACE CULTURE

The notion of compartmentalising work and home lives has long since become outdated. Today more employees work from home than ever before. Childcare responsibilities have changed as people have moved away from their families, either by choice or in their search for work, and of course the sheer speed and pressures of modern day life constantly place demands on workers which lead to them needing greater workplace flexibility.

At the same time as all this has been going on, there has also been a 'revolution' in terms of people's expectations of life as a whole, as well as in their priorities and the things that matter. Money, as we pointed out earlier on in this book, is no longer the driving force for most individuals, and what matters more is creating a life that is rewarding, fulfilling and meaningful in every respect.

In the meantime, however, a great many employers are still stuck in the mindset that 'it's not their job' to pander to the wider needs of their workforces. So long as they are paying their workers a reasonable wage, meeting their obligations to look after their health and safety and being seen to embrace the concepts of equality and diversity, they see themselves as doing an satisfactory job. Unfortunately though, by not creating a workplace culture that meets the broader needs and changed priorities of today's workers, these companies are suffering the effects of cripplingly high employee turnover and the inability to attract great new talent.

What can they do to turn things around? San Francisco event and ticket website company *Eventbrite* offers employees a Zen room to chill out it and allows employees to bring their dog into the office. So many of their employees cycle to work that they have even installed a bike area inside the office to keep all the bikes safe. Here are a few more great ideas to help your business become an employer of choice.

31. EMPLOYEE WORK WEAR

Many different types of company provide work wear or 'uniforms' for their customer-facing employee's, but there is actually no reason why this benefit can't be extended to other employees. As well as providing a great opportunity to publicise your company's corporate identity, this really is a great benefit to your employee's as not only will it save them the cost of buying work clothes, but also having to decide what to wear every morning! You don't have to choose outfits that are drab and feel more like a punishment to wear. Make them fun and your workers will wear them with pride.

Although the provision of employee work wear might not seem like an obvious way to incentivise a workforce, US company *Sweetgreen*, a fast food concept which specialises in fresh, healthy food, has come up with a really imaginative way to use it both as a way to reward their employees for learning and growing with their business, as well as encouraging them to stay with the company. Called 'Shades of Green', their scheme sees every employee receiving green tee shirts of increasingly darker shades each time they celebrate another year's service. The longer they stay, the bigger their collection of tee shirts and other cool stuff grows, and of course the tee shirts themselves act as a status symbol amongst employees and motivate newer workers to stay on and progress.

32. LONG SERVICE

As we're all aware, the days of 'a job for life' have long since passed and the tenure of the average worker has dropped dramatically in recent years. Offering a gold wrist watch for 25 years loyal service in this day and age, therefore, is not only unrealistic, but it does little to motivate or inspire 21st century employees. That doesn't mean to say, however, that rewards for each additional year of service are altogether redundant. It's just a case of 'moving with the times'.

Sweetgreen, who we mentioned in the previous tip, have come up with an inspirational way to build on their tee shirt theme and celebrate their employees' decisions to stay with them for longer periods of time. After one year's service, for example, workers receive a special pair of green *Converse* trainers, and after two years they are rewarded with a green iPod Nano. If they stay for three years, meanwhile, they get a special *Sweetgreen* bike... in green of course!

While a couple of years' service might not seem like much worth celebrating from an employer's point of view, when you bear in mind that many of today's employers are actually wary of applicants who have been in their current job for longer than this, it's hardly surprising that workers feel the need to keep moving on. If you're going to tempt them to stay, therefore, it's vital to find incentives that are cool, attractive and relevant today.

Of course, rewards for extended service don't have to come in the form of 'goods'. Why not consider offering a sabbatical to employees who reach a particular anniversary with your company?

33. SUMMER FRIDAYS

Most employees need a degree of flexibility in their working hours from time to time, enabling them for example to cover childcare arrangements or to look after a sick family member. At other times though, it would just be great to have the flexibility to be able to knock off work early, especially on those long, hot summer days.

Summer Fridays, as well as being a great company perk to offer new job candidates, are also a great way to boost the productivity and morale of existing employees. By being allowed to leave at noon or lunchtime, they benefit from an extended weekend and typically return feeling happier and more refreshed. Those extra few hours on a Friday afternoon can also contribute greatly to reducing stress levels and the amount of sick leave that employees might otherwise take as a result.

Of course, the work isn't just going to go away while employees are off sunning themselves but, depending on the nature of your business, you could either stipulate that employees must finish their work before they leave - it's amazing how eight hours' work can be fitted into four hours without any reduction in quality if employees have the motivation to do so - or let them work an hour extra on each of the other days to make up the difference.

34. THE 9/80 SCHEME

With today's busy lifestyles taking such a toll on workers, being able to offer year-round flexibility to working hours can be a tremendous way to encourage company loyalty and keep employees motivated. Many US companies in particular are leading the way in terms of offering flexible working schemes, and some are even seeing benefits from cutting the number of hours worked per week!

Online tech school *Treehouse* which is based in Florida and employs 55 people, has a working week that lasts from Monday through to Thursday and still pays its workers for 19 days' holiday plus a whole two weeks at Christmas. The company doesn't even try to make up the 'lost' time from giving its employees three-day weekends, but still benefits because their employees reward them with immense company loyalty. Undoubtedly this huge incentive offered by *Treehouse* means that they are able to hire some of the best people in their field, and because these employees knuckle down and get on with the job without wasting any time when they are there, there simply isn't the need to claw back the one day a week.

If three-day weekends feel a step too far though, you could instead offer the chance for your employees to take alternate Fridays off under the 9/80 working hours scheme. Basically, the 9/80 work schedule involves working nine hours a day from Mondays through to Thursdays and then either doing an eight-hour day or taking the day off on alternate Fridays, so completing 80 hours of work in nine days instead of 10.

In order to avoid the situation where your business looks like the Marie Celeste every other Friday, you'll want to stagger the days off so that at least half of your employee's are available. Alternatively, you could still stagger the days off and have some employees working Monday to Thursday with alternate Fridays off while others work Tuesday to Friday with alternate Mondays off. That way you can always ensure that 75% of your workforce are present on any given day.

35. LATE WORKERS

Sometimes long days and late nights are inevitable and so it's likely that people will need feeding and transport home. *Zocdoc* and *Tumblr* both have a clear policy on this - work past 8pm and that means dinner is on the company and a cab ride home too. By having a clear policy in these areas it demonstrates to employees that their extra effort is recognised.

36. REMOTE WORKING

There are many roles where some or all of the work that employee does can be done remotely from home. This works really well for almost any desk based job role and offers many advantages:

The employee saves on time spent commuting (just 30 mins each way plus time parking and so on add's up to 300-400 hours per year - who wouldn't want to get that time back?)

1. The company could benefit from big savings on office costs - rent, heat, light, maintenance etc.
2. Productivity has been shown to jump because of the reduction in interruptions

3. Companies are not restricted to hiring talent from their commutable catchment area - the best talent can be hired anywhere there is an internet connection
4. Other talent pools will open up - young mothers without the time to commute between school drop-off and pick-up. People living in remote areas. People in other countries

Not convinced? In the period 2005 - 2011 remote working soared 73% in the U.S.A. Major companies utilising remote working include *IBM, Intel, British Telecom, HSBC, Unilever, Mercedes Benz, Virgin Atlantic, Github, McKinsey & Co* and many many others.

During the period since 1995, *IBM* has reduced its office space by 78 million square feet through its teleworking program and cites annual savings of $100m!

Clearly remote working is not suitable for all roles but well worth considering.

* Source for section: *Remote*, by Jason Fried & David Heinemeier Hannson

37. SOCIAL & CHARITABLE INITIATIVES

In years gone by, it used to be primarily those in the older age brackets who were especially interested in doing charitable work and giving something back to their local communities or the world at large. Nowadays, however, increasing numbers of younger people have highly developed social consciences and a desire to make their world a better place. Why not give your workforce the opportunity then, to use part of their work time to focus on the social or charitable initiatives that they are most interested in?

Letting employees work on 'good deeds' that will benefit worthy causes provides two significant benefits for employers. First of all, it gives their workers that deep sense of fulfilment and meaning that so many desire nowadays. As a by-product though, it also raises the profile of the company as one which is socially aware and active. Given the growing interest in Corporate Social Responsibility operating in this way is likely to have a more and more positive impact over time.

Outdoor brand *Patagonia* offers an 'Environmental Internship' programme - where it allows employees to work full-time, on full salary and benefits for a cause they are passionate about. Over 750 employees have taken this opportunity working for causes as varied as the preservation of wolves in the Grand Canyon and wilderness sustainability in Nevada.

38. CREATE TIME FOR CREATIVITY

As we discussed in tactic number 25, workers often have some great 'off the cuff' ideas on how to make their own jobs easier or how to improve the business. Two of the main reasons why these ideas typically never come into the open though, are:

1. Because employees don't have any confidence that they will be taken seriously, and...
2. Because unless they do it in their own time, employees don't usually have the time or head space at work to properly think their ideas through or to make them as good as they could be

A great way to counteract both of these obstacles and really tap into the creativity of your workforce is to give everyone in the company a day away from the office. Spend the time on devising, creating and researching a way to make their job easier, faster or more productive, or come up with a plan for improving the business in a wider sense.

Naturally, this day shouldn't just be treated like a day off by anyone involved, so make it clear to your employees that they will each have to present their idea on their return. Once the presentations have taken place (you could perhaps do this on a team or departmental basis, rather than expecting employees to stand up and present to the entire organisation), everyone then gets to vote for the best idea. The final decision as to which idea should be taken forward should ultimately be left to the manager, and the person whose winning idea it was should of course receive the appropriate reward and recognition.

39. PERSONAL MILESTONES

Especially in the case of larger organisations which tend to be more anonymous, it can sometimes be all too easy to lose sight of the fact that all those people who turn up for work every day are actually individuals in their own right, with lives and interests outside of the workplace. As well as the bad stuff that we all have to face from time to time, these people also enjoy successes and reach important milestones in their lives, although often these are completely overlooked by the people with whom they spend the majority of their time... their bosses and colleagues.

Making employees feel like 'part of the family', or at the very least like something more than just a number, really takes very little effort or money. There are numerous opportunities throughout the year to show them how valued they are as people by helping them celebrate personal occasions such as:

- Birthdays
- Weddings
- Engagements
- The births of their new babies
- Passing exams
- Passing their driving tests
- Winning sports competitions or awards related to their outside hobbies and interests

Although you might want to be a little circumspect about announcing Dorothy's 60th birthday to the entire organisation (many people prefer to keep their age a closely-guarded secret for professional reasons), publicising a special event or personal achievement within an individual's team is a great way to help them celebrate and get everyone involved.

Don't automatically expect one of the individual's colleagues to sort out a greetings card that everyone can sign, but take responsibility for it yourself or assign the task to a manager, otherwise it might simply be overlooked. Also, why not arrange for cakes and drinks for everyone to enjoy, or organise some group photographs to be taken to really make it an occasion.

Helping employees to celebrate personal events is a great way to make them feel recognised, but for it to be truly successful the team or group needs to be small enough that everyone at least knows each other, even if they're not well-acquainted. Who knows though... by the end of the celebration the team might all know one another a great deal better!

40. 'EVENTS' PARTIES

Throughout the course of the average year, there's usually at least one big, live televised event that nobody wants to miss, whether it's a world-class sports fixture or a royal wedding. Rather than leaving your employees to feel as though they're missing out, why not lay on some food and drink, shut down operations to a minimum level and invite your employees to the canteen so that they can watch on a big screen? If you need to leave a skeleton cover, then arrange for people to attend in relays so that everyone gets to enjoy the fun for at least part of the time.

As with many of the other tips that we've looked at so far, allowing employees to watch and celebrate big events has more than one positive outcome for employers. First of all, it acts as a treat or reward that will be appreciated by all who take part. Secondly though, it helps to reduce levels of absenteeism which often tend to rocket on the days when such events take place.

Bringing everyone into the canteen or board room and organising big screens and catering has become popular when there is a major sporting event happening in another time zone. These events could take the form of team breakfasts together, evening parties or even extended lunch-breaks.

Another thing that might be worth considering is giving people access to a television when events such as big natural disasters or significant world events are being reported on the news. Often people catch wind of these through news updates on their phones or through calls from friends and family, and especially if your employee's have loved ones in the area where the event is taking place, not knowing the details of what is happening can be extremely distressing and distracting for them.

41. KIDS IN THE WORKPLACE

Kids' workplace days teach children and young adults a number of very useful lessons, about:

- How adults serve a useful role in society
- The links between the worlds of education and work and what they need to do to successfully make the move from one to the other
- What certain roles are like in real life, rather than as portrayed on the television or in films

If organised well though, they can also be a tremendous amount of fun and provide opportunities for some great parent/child bonding experiences.

Most businesses use 'Take Our Daughters and Sons to Work Day' as an opportunity to host an annual kids' workplace day, and often schools support the event by getting children to write about and share their learning experiences with their teachers and classmates. The day can be a great opportunity for your employees' children to see what their parents do and actually take part in their roles, as well as to move around other departments in the organisation and gain a better appreciation of valuable workplace concepts such as team working and co-operation.

Ideally you will want to set an age range for the youngsters taking part. Many companies use 8-18 as their guide, not only because younger children are less likely to benefit from the experience, but also because their low boredom thresholds typically create more disruption and because looking after their health and safety tends to be more of a challenge. Even when restricted to the 8-18s though, it's important to include some of the more exciting parts of your business in the day's activities and to be well-prepared with special 'work packs' for the children that will help them to learn and be enjoyable for them to complete.

Knowing that Mum or Dad has to go to work every day and actually being able to see their work environment and get an inside view of what they do all day are two completely different things. By holding kids' workplace days, your company could be giving your employees' children valuable insights into an aspect of life that they wouldn't otherwise be able to appreciate, and helping them to put their lives into context in a broader sense. They are also a great chance to let your workers show off their kids and for your employees to appreciate one another as more than just fellow workers. *Mothercare* invites employees to bring their kids to the office just before Christmas and puts on a special lunch for everyone in the canteen, before sending them all home early.

42. HOMEWORK HELPLINE

Gone are the days when Mum used to stay at home and look after the children while Dad went out to work. A significant proportion of today's workforces are made up of working parents, most of whom find themselves juggling their home and workplace responsibilities, and most of whom suffer at least periodic bouts of guilt about the fact that they can't be there to support their children with fairly basic things such as helping them with their homework.

As we keep reiterating throughout this book, one of the fundamental keys to engaging a workforce is by recognising each individual as more than just an employee and creating a culture which supports them in ways that contribute to making their lives as a whole more manageable. One way that technology giant *Intel* has approached this in relation to helping workers with parental responsibilities is by investing in the innovative education service provided by *Tutor.com*.

Tutor.com offers a variety of live, online, on-demand learning solutions for both students and professionals, and *Intel* subscribes to a 'homework helpline' for employees' children who are in grades 4-12 and aged roughly from 9-17 years. The service is completely free of charge to employees and their children can access professional tutors specialising in a whole range of subjects at any time of the day or night and seven days a week.

At the same time as providing the children with a readily-accessible source of help, this benefit is of course invaluable to employees in that it helps to alleviate some of the stress and the guilt commonly experienced when they aren't able to get home in time to help their youngsters with homework. In addition though, it provides solutions which are relevant to today's teaching methods and that children can more readily understand. After all, we've all experienced the frustration of trying to show children how to solve a problem using methods that we were taught years ago, only to find that we might just as well be speaking an entirely different language!

43. ALTERNATIVE TRANSPORT

Perhaps more so than any that have gone before, today's younger generations of workers are genuinely concerned about making their world a better place to live. It goes without saying, therefore, that employers who share their concerns and values offer a better prospect to new candidates who are considering joining their companies and existing employees alike.

Tackling environmental issues is, of course, becoming ever more important in a world where scarce resources are being depleted at alarming rates. By rewarding employees who forsake the convenience of using their own cars to travel to and from the workplace, employers have a great opportunity to make a positive environmental impact at the same time as acknowledging and sharing the concerns of their workers. Encourage and incentivise employees to walk to work, travel by bike, use public transport or set up car sharing schemes.

Walking or travelling to work by bicycle are great ways to introduce higher levels of physical activity into employees' lifestyles too, which means that you build a stronger and healthier workforce. As we mentioned previously, another huge benefit lies in the fact that companies whose cultures demonstrate an active interest in addressing environmental concerns are also far more likely to appeal to customers and clients.

44. OFFICE CONCIERGE

Because time is the greatest enemy of most working people caught between their various roles and responsibilities in life, any employer initiative which helps to free up valuable minutes and hours is likely to be welcomed with open arms. One such initiative that you might want to consider is providing an office concierge service.

Setting up an office concierge service is a great opportunity to leverage the organisational skills of, for example, reception staff, and it can help save your employees the time and hassle involved in arranging necessary but time-consuming activities ranging from booking their cars in for cleaning or valeting to organising dry cleaning and ironing services. As these are chores which would normally have to be dealt with in their lunch breaks or leisure time, effectively a concierge service can help to free up more of your employees' time for the fun things in life.

Although this initiative won't necessarily save your employee's money, you could of course negotiate discounts with local businesses for pointing your employee's in their direction.

45. SHARE A CAUSE

Starting up a social enterprise scheme with neighbouring businesses can provide employees with some wonderful opportunities to give back to their communities and contribute directly to addressing social and environmental issues. In addition, however, it can also significantly improve networking opportunities, which could in turn lead to improved business prospects.

The type of social enterprise scheme that you could become involved in is really only limited by imagination. International brand consultants

Wolff Olins, for example, were instrumental in setting up The Honey Club, a product-led initiative which centres around beekeeping. Participating companies place hives on the rooftops of their business premises and produce local honey which is taken along to exhibitions and tasting events, and they even hold 'hackdays' in local restaurants where enthusiasts can get together.

As well as being a valuable tool in terms of generating a renewed sense of local community, The Honey Club has also proved to be highly effective in terms of attracting great new talent to *Wolff Olins*' business, once again demonstrating the importance of sharing the values and concerns of today's workers.

46. SKUNK WORKS

Creativity and innovation are absolutely key to staying alive in today's markets, many of which have reached saturation point. Developing creative ideas within the confines of the typically strict processes and regulations of most organisations, however, can be virtually impossible. That's where a skunk works comes in.

Originating from a *Lockheed* initiative during World War II, the term 'skunk works' is essentially applied to a small group of people who are taken outside of their normal working environment and given exceptional freedom to work on a high priority, top secret research and development project. The concept has been adopted by high-profile companies such as *Google* and was also used by Steve Jobs at *Apple* for the development of the *Macintosh* computer. Although it lends itself particularly well to the technology industry, any business which is looking to develop innovative ideas can set up its own skunk works to drive things forward quickly.

Not surprisingly, skunk works are hugely attractive to the high calibre employees who should be selected to take part in them, as well as to potential job candidates looking for great new opportunities in organisations that will permit them to develop their skills and talents. As skunk works team members are typically paid highly for their contribution to the project, there is also a great financial incentive for your best workers to be involved, and they can be assured access to special resources which might not ordinarily be available to them.

47. E-MAIL EMBARGO

Acknowledging the difficulties that employees face and the things that get in the way of their being able to get through their workloads and still leave time for projects that will develop them, is absolutely crucial if you are going to keep them motivated and engaged. Ask what holds them back most, and the sheer quantity of e-mails that hit their inboxes is almost certain to appear on their lists.

It is estimated that 50-75% of the e-mail traffic in most companies today is internal, but while most employees might consider e-mail to be quick and convenient, in fact it can waste huge amounts of time at best, and at worst can create confusion and damage employee relations. So, why not try an e-mail embargo to give everyone a break and to find out whether your company might not benefit from alternative methods of communication?

There are actually several ways that you could introduce a ban on internal e-mail. You could, for example, prohibit the use of e-mails within the same department, or bring in a company-wide ban for a period of a week. Either way, the effect will almost certainly be that your employee's will talk to each other more and everyone will spend far less time writing and reading messages which are often far too complicated to warrant anything less than a face-to-face conversation.

Another option is to replace internal e-mail with an instant messaging facility to encourage short, quick responses. The ability to hold simultaneous conversations with colleagues, take part in group conferences and share documents can make instant messaging a highly flexible but much less onerous and time-consuming alternative to traditional e-mails.

Of course, ultimately most businesses are not going to want to dispense with internal e-mail altogether, and in fact one experiment which was carried out by the Chief Executive of *Learning is Leadership*, an organisation devoted to tapping the full potential of leaders, teams and organisations, revealed four particular uses of e-mail that did enhance productivity, namely:

- In conveying simple, defined information such as meeting agendas or directions to a location, where no questions are being asked and there's nothing confusing about the content of the message
- Delegating clear administrative tasks which again don't raise questions or necessitate any discussion, such as asking for a document to be sent or that an appointment be scheduled with a particular individual
- Sending a document as agreed in a previous conversation
- Documenting or summarising a completed conversation to ensure clarity. In some cases the e-mail need contain nothing more than, "*As discussed, please find attached the minutes of our project meeting*," whilst in others they might start with something like, "*Here is what I understood from the performance review that I have just taken part in*."

48. BUSINESS AWARDS TEAM

Especially when faced with the daily challenge of the job, it can sometimes be easy for employees to lose sight of what's good about the business they work for. One great way to counteract this, however, is by appointing a business awards team which is responsible for entering the company into award competitions.

At the same time as focussing employees on all the really positive elements and achievements of the company, entering awards is also a fantastic way to encourage employees to generate fresh, new ideas to bring into your business. In addition, there is every likelihood that, over time, your company will reach the finals and even start to win awards which will not only have the benefit of creating awareness, publicity and praise for your business, but will also have a hugely motivational effect on those who work for you.

If you're looking for business awards to enter and are a startup or new business venture, try taking a look at the business awards and competitions list at *entrepreneurhandbook.co.uk/competitions-award/*. Celebrating the success of businesses around Europe, meanwhile, are the European Business Awards, details of which can be found at *businessawardseurope.com/about*. Other great places to start though, are with local and regional award competitions (just type the name of your county and 'business awards' into your preferred search engine) and those run by any professional bodies or organisations affiliated to your particular trade or business.

49. BREAKFAST BOOK CLUB

Helping workers to feel inspired is absolutely crucial if they are going to stay motivated to consistently deliver of their best and to remain loyal to your business. Providing inspiration though, is one area where many managers and leaders tend to fall short of the mark. Car giants *Mercedes Benz*, however, have come up with a simple and yet highly effective way to encourage their workers to reach for the heights.

Within the Financial Services division of *Mercedes Benz*, the CEO hosts a monthly 'You Don't Have to Read the Book' book club, during which each of the company executives in turn presents a book that he or she has read and discusses how the book has influenced their career or their life. The benefit of these breakfast book clubs is twofold. Firstly, they inspire employees to learn and bring about positive change in their own professional and personal lives. Secondly, they also encourage the company's executives to continue their learning and education, if for no other reason than to ensure that they have a great story to tell when their turn comes around.

50. MAGAZINE SUBSCRIPTIONS

Business journals and magazines offer a great way to stay in touch with what's happening within your particular field or industry, but often the cost of these publications can put them out of the reach of everyone but the highest-paid employees. So, why not demonstrate your commitment to the learning and development of your workforce by investing in subscriptions to the most relevant journals within your industry?

There are two ways that you can go about providing magazine subscriptions within your business. Either your company could subscribe to a whole range of publications or you could pay for subscriptions for individual employees. If you go for the former option, place copies of the journals in communal and rest areas where they are easily accessible to everyone. Either way though, your company or employee's could choose from publications that focus on:

- Your own company's trade or industry
- The particular market sector that you're involved in and any related consumer magazines
- The sectors or industries that your clients are involved in

Professional journals and magazines not only offer a less formal approach to learning and development, but because they are published on a regular basis, they help readers to stay at the forefront of their industries. Advertisements can help point your business in the direction of new or better suppliers or innovative training opportunities and courses, and of course the content itself can stimulate ideas for new products, services or business processes, as well as providing examples of best industry practice which could be incorporated into your own business.

51. THANK YOU DAYS

Whether at a personal or professional level, at home or within the workplace, we all have an innate desire to feel appreciated. A simple 'Thank You' goes a very long way in terms of letting us know that our efforts have not gone unnoticed and is instrumental in motivating us to give of our best. Especially in business though, this basic courtesy is frequently overlooked. Instead, a culture of expectation is allowed to develop and predominate, with the end result that everyone from customers and clients to company employees and colleagues ultimately feel undervalued.

Kicking off the process of developing a culture of appreciation can be a challenge if saying "Thank You" isn't something that your company is accustomed to. By designating a day on which each employee is asked to send a specified number of Thank You cards to both internal and external customers, however, you can encourage employees to start focussing on the positive impacts that their colleagues make on their day-to-day roles and responsibilities, as well as on showing appreciation to the customers and clients who could, let's face it, have chosen to take their business elsewhere.

Thank You days are inexpensive and easy to implement, and not only do they have a direct impact on the recipient, but they also promote a culture of appreciation around the entire business.

52. PAIN-FREE CHILDCARE

One of the biggest concerns for workers of both genders lies in how to successfully manage the overlap between their professional lives and their personal lives. Key to this, of course, is childcare. Working parents are not only faced with the challenge of finding affordable childcare, but perhaps more importantly, of finding childcare providers that they can trust. Without a practical solution to this dilemma, often they can find themselves feeling distracted from their professional duties and in need of far greater flexibility in the workplace, neither of which are productive for employers.

Helping to take the financial and/or organisational pain out of childcare arrangements is one of the most impactful things an employer can do, and there are several different ways that this can be achieved. You can either:

- Subsidise the cost of the childcare arrangements that working parents make with the providers of their choice
- Set up an on-site childcare facility where children can be dropped off and picked up at the beginning and end of the day and where parents can visit their children during their lunch breaks, or
- Set up a joint venture with a reputable and trustworthy childcare provider in the local vicinity of your business, and perhaps even arrange a pick-up and drop-off service from the office

Having that additional peace of mind that comes with knowing that their children are in a safe environment and being well cared-for can typically mean that employees are more productive and lose fewer days from work. Even though subsidising or providing childcare clearly comes at a cost to employers, often this is partially or wholly offset by the consequential gains. In addition, it's another huge incentive for talented young workers to join your organisation.

PART 6
HEALTH AND WELL BEING

Good health and physical and psychological well-being are not just fundamental to a productive work life, but of course to a rich and happy life in general. Employers that provide schemes and initiatives aimed at improving the physical and mental condition of their workforce benefit twofold. At the same time as 'feathering their own nests' by reducing absenteeism and insurance costs, they ensure an overall boost to their workers' quality of life. In addition, because they are seen as caring organisations by both employees and customers or clients, they often benefit from better professional reputations.

Here are just a few ways that your business could reap the rewards of taking a more active involvement in the health and well-being of your workers.

53. CONFIDENTIAL HELPLINE

No worker can be expected to be at the top of his or her game in the workplace if they are weighed down either by professional or personal concerns. For this reason, many of today's companies provide a confidential employee helpline that employees can call to discuss work issues, or anything else that might be troubling them.

In order for your employee's to feel truly confident in your company helpline service you will want to use an outside provider. No matter whether an employee wants to discuss a personal or professional issue, there's always going to be a huge leap of trust in picking up the phone and most workers won't feel at all comfortable in knowing that their concerns are being heard by another company employee.

Of course, you as a business can decide the extent of the provider's remit. You might want to restrict it, for example, to dealing solely with work-related problems such as:

- Workplace bullying
- Internal security issues, or
- Gripes and complaints

You could even use it as a forum for collecting suggestions or a conduit for giving praise that employees don't want to provide publicly.

In many cases though, company helplines provide a wider service which offers support and advice in relation to personal problems too. These might include, for example:

- Financial problems
- Health issues, or
- Family issues

Despite their potential for impacting negatively on workplace performance, most employees would shy away from discussing issues such as these with their employers directly. After all, who would want to admit to their manager or HR representative that they had a problem with gambling or alcoholism when doing so might at the very least cause their judgement or character to be called into question, and in the very worst case could lead to their dismissal?

If you don't want to go down the line of setting up a full employee helpline, another option might be to set up a private website where employees could leave suggestions, register complaints, give praise and so on. Do be mindful, however, that even in making use of a service such as this, most employees will want to feel confident that their input is anonymous.

54. PERSONAL SUPPORT

Whether employees feel supported by their employer during times of need is likely to have a strong impact on their levels of engagement.

The effects of bereavement, family illnesses and other types of personal traumas, after all, can't be compartmentalised and fitted conveniently into the hours outside 9-5, and those who suffer these experiences in their lives need the support of everyone around them, including their employer.

The type of support that your company chooses to offer could include any or all of the following:

- Special leave with pay
- Financial support
- Professional counselling at the company's expense
- The provision of domestic help or support
- Weight Watchers membership

What is important though, is that your business does something to create a culture of caring and understanding and that employees know that they can turn to you in times of trouble.

Of course, all of the above suggestions come at a cost to employers and whilst it may not be easy for many businesses to afford them at the time, they are invariably rewarded further down the line through greater effort and loyalty. Companies that support their employee's through personal crises also tend to benefit because their lead effectively fosters a 'pay it forward' culture amongst employees.

To give an indication of just how valued employer support can be, consider the funeral concierge service offered by North American company *Everest*. The Everest employee program has proved so popular it boasts 15 million people who have signed up through their employee programme!

55. EMPLOYEE SECURITY

Although most businesses today are only too aware of meeting their obligations with respect to health and safety, all too often they see their responsibilities as beginning and ending at the front door of their premises. In truly embracing the spirit of looking after the health and well-being of your employee's though, it's often necessary to look a bit further.

Think, for example, about the area around your business premises, and in particular the car parks. Are they brightly-lit and covered by security cameras so that employees feel safe when leaving your building? Or could you perhaps enlist the help of security people in escorting people to their vehicles?

For those employees who use public transport to get to and from work, sometimes the walk to the station or bus stop can be intimidating, especially if the business is in a remote or run-down location and during the dark winter months. Again, think about what your business could do to ensure that they get there safely. How about offering a free shuttle service between your premises and some of the main local departure points for example?

In the case of employees who work regular late shifts, as well as those who only occasionally stay late to help the business out, always lay on transport to get them to or from their place of work. If your company can't stretch to its own dedicated transport service, then set up an agreement with a reputable local taxi service that can be put at your employee's disposal. Whatever you spend in securing the personal safety of your workers is minimal compared to the loss of your business reputation should something terrible happen to them on their journeys to and from work.

56. HEALTHY DIETS

Although it would be hard to ignore advice concerning the impact of poor diets on general health and well-being, surprisingly few people are truly aware of just how devastating these can be. Even if it doesn't lead to illness as such, poor nutrition is responsible for feelings of sluggishness and lack of vigour, and of course this has hugely detrimental effects on productivity.

When UK company *Chemistry* looked into why business grew steadily throughout the first part of the year but then fizzled out as the year progressed, it turned out that the problem was down to sheer exhaustion. The company's response to the problem was, first of all, to increase each employee's allocation of paid holiday and make sure that this was used. Alongside this they also employed a nutritionist to find out whether their workers' diets were having any appreciable impact on their levels of energy. The discovery that none of their employee's were eating properly.

Taking matters into their own hands, *Chemistry* began spending around £1,200 every month on food for its employee's and worked with the nutritionist to provide cooking classes for its employees. These lessons taught employees how to prepare cheap, healthy meals and the whole experience was even livened up with the organisation's own version of *Come Dine With Me* in which two employees cooked a meal for the group once a week and were marked on taste and nutritional value, as well as on presentation. The knock-on effect has been a complete change in the workers' attitudes to food, with many reporting weight loss, as well as a heightened interest in exercise. Six months after setting up the nutrition programme, the company's orders doubled from £2 million to £4 million!

57. HEALTHY DIETS 2

Given the clear benefits to employers and employees alike of healthier and more nutritional diets, another couple of options that you might want to consider are hiring a breakfast or lunchtime chef to cater for your employees or providing your employee's with free, healthy meals.

Two companies which have started up similar initiatives are *Clif Bar* and *Sweetgreen*, both of which are in the wholesome, healthy food business. *Clif Bar* founder, Gary Erickson, actually employs his grandmother Kali to run Kali's Kitchen at the firm's head office. Working with local organic farmers, Kali sources the best ingredients and produces healthy, affordable meals for all the employees at the office.

At *Sweetgreen*, meanwhile, each employee receives a salad on every shift that they work. So successful has their initiative been that the company's People Manager noticed that the sizes of uniform shirts being ordered by their employee's were getting smaller the longer the employee's were with the company!

58. WELL BEING HEALTH CHECKS

Like everything in life, the state of employee health and well-being is something that changes over time. A worker who is fit and well one month might be anything but in the month that follows. Taking regular stock of how your employees are doing, therefore, can be a great way, not only of recognising and dealing with current issues, but also of nipping potential problems in the bud.

The question of who should take responsibility for monitoring employees well-being can, however, be a tricky one. Although most would agree that the company CEO should ultimately be responsible for ensuring that employees are doing okay, it isn't usually practicable for one person to deal with the individual concerns of an entire workforce. The answer then, is to help managers with carrying out this task.

The key thing about employee welfare and well-being is that it encompasses so many different areas and the overall well-being of one individual employee could be affected by a variety of factors. Therefore if a company leaves the responsibility for employees well-being solely in the hands of managers whose primary interest might be in employees reward and recognition, there is the danger that occupational health or health and safety issues, for example, might not be properly addressed. What is important then, is to provide managers with the input and advice of more specialised personnel within the business, such as members of the HR team, occupational health workers or health and safety representatives.

U.S businesses *J.M Smucker* and *Angie's List* take this to another level by offering $1,000 to employees who quit smoking, free health screenings, health fairs and even cover the cost of prescription drugs.

Make employee well-being checks a priority within your business by having managers schedule them in regularly. If not, you can almost guarantee that the first they will know of a problem will be when it's already had chance to impact significantly on the individual employees' professional and personal lives.

PART 7
MOVEMENT EQUALS MOTIVATION

As we've already seen, the benefits to business of having fit, healthy workers are many. Not only does encouraging healthier lifestyles lead to reduced levels of absenteeism and lower health insurance bills, but healthy employees contribute to a much more positive and energetic business culture which is more attractive to current workers, potential employees, clients and customers alike.

While healthy eating is an important facet of achieving and maintaining the peak of physical and mental condition, of course physical activity is also key. Here are a few ideas to help get your workforce moving!

59. OFFICE GYM OR CLUB MEMBERSHIP

While there are businesses such as *Nike* who are able to support their people with amazing facilities such as on-site gyms, courts for every sport you can think of, climbing walls, swimming pools and even a *Tour De France* simulator these are, of course, the exception rather than the rule.

Providing free memberships for employees at a nearby gym or health club, however, is a realistic and affordable alternative for most businesses. Especially if the facility is close enough for employees to be able to use it at lunchtime as well as before or after work, the take-up is likely to be good and the benefits for employers and their workers more pronounced.

If your business is lucky enough to be one of those which has its own on-site gym, then you could encourage even greater use by following the lead of advertising agency and brand builders *HZDG*. They have gone one step further by employing a personal trainer to come in twice a week and run different classes, as well as to help employees develop individual training plans to keep them on track to meet their goals.

60. PAID WORKOUT / FITNESS TIME

Many people are full of the best intentions when it comes to exercising. Trying to cram a fitness regime into today's busy lifestyles though, is typically a struggle, and all but the most dedicated fitness fanatics tend to fall by the wayside. As an employer, therefore, the keys to encouraging better health within your workforce are:

1. To give your employee's easy access to the fitness resources they need, and

2. To make the necessary time available to them for exercising

At Italian 'wellness' company *Technogym*, every day is a workout day for the majority of employees. Not only have chairs been largely replaced by fabric-covered exercise balls of the type used in gyms to strengthen core muscles, but employees have a mandatory two-hour lunch break during which they're encouraged to use the company's on-site gym. Unlike most workers who are restricted to a 30 minute lunch break, *Technogym's* employees have plenty of time to exercise, shower and eat before returning to their desks.

Technogym's approach to fostering improved health and well-being works on two levels: First of all, the use of exercise balls in place of chairs has brought about a dramatic reduction in the number of cases of back pain, the single biggest contributor of time lost from the workplace. Secondly, the provision of easily-accessible exercise facilities along with the time to use them, effectively removes the barriers that would otherwise deter employees from taking part in a programme of exercise.

As we keep reiterating throughout this book, whilst there is a cost attached to an initiative such as this, the experience of companies who invest in the health and well-being of their employee's is that it pales into insignificance when measured against the resulting reduction in absenteeism and increase in performance. For the employees themselves, of course, the improvements in their overall health, strength and stamina don't just impact on their working lives, but overflow into their personal lives too.

If you are in the sailing, snowboard, surfing business or any business related to an activity that needs certain weather conditions why not take *Burton Snowboards* lead: everyday in the winter season they have more than 2 feet of snow fall is an automatic snow day. As long as the work gets done (at some point) they want people to get on the mountain together and enjoy the great conditions.

61. SUBSIDISE PEOPLE'S FAVOURITE ACTIVITIES

With any type of employee reward and recognition scheme, it's vital to understand what appeals to one employee might be another individual's worst nightmare. In fostering a culture of physical and mental well-being, this is something that communication developers *Twilio* have truly taken on board under the banner of 'Limber bodies make limber minds'.

Rather than restricting its fitness offering to gym membership, *Twilio* subsidises whatever fitness activity its employee's want to become involved in. It doesn't matter whether employees favour kickboxing or ballroom dancing, if the activity contributes to improved physical condition, then the company will support it.

As simple as this idea might be, it's actually a stroke of genius because of course no-one is going to stick with a fitness activity if they don't enjoy it. Let your workers choose what they feel passionate about and not only will they keep at it, but they'll reap the benefits too.

62. SPORTS EVENT BUDGET

The very nature of sport and fitness activities means that it's quite common for participants to want to push themselves further. They might, for example, start off with a gentle daily jog, but before long develop aspirations to take part in a marathon. One way to help and encourage employees to reach their peak of physical fitness, as well as to show off their sporting prowess, is to follow the example of *Clif Bar*, the American energy bar company that we mentioned earlier, by providing each employee with an allowance to cover entry costs for races, events and competitions. You could even extend your contribution to take into account participants' travelling costs or provide them with free kit. Better still, show them how proud you are by hiring someone to photograph or film their success!

Recent years have seen increasing numbers of people take part in charity fundraising events such as the *Race for Life* organised by *Cancer Research UK*. Another great way to support employees in their quest for fitness, therefore, might be to offer sponsorship to those who take part. Not only is this likely to encourage higher levels of participation, but it also allows employees to work towards their more philanthropic and social goals and derive satisfaction from the feeling that they're doing their bit to make the world a better place.

The benefits to the company and it's clients of a workforce which is strong, healthy and has stamina is indisputable. The approach to creating a culture of health and well-being, however, is one that can only be decided by each individual company. While many prefer a more 'softly, softly' style which encourages and incentivises workers to improve their overall physical condition, others have taken a slightly harder line. US bike company *Trek*, for instance, uses tactics such as levying a 'Twinkie tax' on junk food purchased from their company cafe, tying the contributions that it makes to health insurance schemes to mandatory health checks and insisting on annual risk assessments for their most at-risk employees.

Whichever approach you choose though, what is important is that you do make a choice. Physical activity, after all, doesn't just improve people's physical condition. The release of all those 'feel-good' hormones has immensely beneficial effects on their mental condition as well. When you bear in mind that stress is responsible for the loss of more than 225 million working days every year in the US, isn't it time your business made employees health and well-being a priority?

PART 8
WORKPLACE ENVIRONMENT

Most employees spend at least half of their waking hours between Monday and Friday in the workplace, and another good chunk of time commuting to and fro. Clearly if the environment that they are expected to work in is uncomfortable or, worse still, unclean, they're hardly going to be racing in each morning eager to start the day.

Here, therefore, are a few tips on how to make sure your office is a place that workers don't mind spending time in.

63. ENSURE YOUR WORKPLACE AND EMPLOYEES AREAS ARE FUNCTIONAL

As harsh as this might sound, any organisation that doesn't provide a functional workplace and employees facilities really doesn't deserve any employees, let alone the best. After all, the provision of basic amenities is a clear demonstration of the respect and regard in which an employer holds his employees.

While the quality of workplace facilities will naturally be dependent upon available budget, don't be tempted to skimp if you can afford something better. Not only do your customers and clients judge you on the provisions you make for your employee's, but so too do those great new job candidates that you're trying to attract!

If your business is one of those that still chooses its office chairs according to where an employee sits in the company hierarchy, then think again. Badly-designed seating is responsible for back problems which cost organisations vast sums of money every year through high health insurance premiums and lost work days.

So, what are the basic facilities that you need to consider?

- Good chairs – your office employees are spending the best part of eight hours a day sat at their desks and there's nothing worse than being in a chair that's uncomfortable or working at a desk that's at the wrong height – in fact either of these things can cause long-term health problems such as repetitive strain injuries that your company could be liable for. Always provide ergonomically-designed height-adjustable chairs and do remember that you have a legal obligation to provide specially adapted furniture for disabled employees or even, for example, to accommodate someone who has longer than average legs! Alternatively, follow *Technogym's* example and opt for exercise balls instead. Because these don't offer a stable surface on which to sit, your employees will effectively get a full-body workout while they're working.

- Proper Desks - The type of desks you choose will also have an important bearing on the comfort and health of your workers. Make sure that they're large enough to accommodate computers, files and anything else that your employees use during the course of the working day, and that everything can be placed within easy reach without stretching or twisting into awkward positions. Also, in order to avoid repetitive strain type injuries, you need to ensure that the right body alignment can be achieved between desk and chair. Remember, when using a computer keyboard, forearms should be parallel to thighs and the user must be able to place his or her feet flat on the floor.

  Height-adjustable standing desks are becoming increasingly popular in many office environments, not least because reports indicate that spending too much time sitting down significantly lowers the metabolic rate and increases the risk of heart disease, blood clots on the brain, diabetes and even certain types of cancer. Perhaps surprisingly, workers who are provided with them offer prefer standing desks to the more conventional sitting variety and for employers they can be a much cheaper alternative.

- Great lighting - again, the quality of the lighting in your work areas isn't just an aesthetic thing. Poor quality lighting can cause discomfort, eye strain and headaches and in the worst cases can even be the cause of accidents.
- Personal storage - making personal lockers available for your employee's not only ensures that the work environment stays clear, tidy and free from trip hazards, but it also provides essential security for their personal possessions
- Employee kitchen and dining area - not all companies have the space for a dedicated employees canteen or restaurant and many employees prefer to bring their own lunches with them anyway, so always make sure that you provide a kitchen area where they can prepare and store food as well as make hot drinks during the course of the day. Make sure that these facilities are clean and well-equipped. Also, ensure that there are adequate numbers of tables and chairs available so that workers don't feel obliged to take their meals back to their desks to eat.
- Social areas - whether you screen off part of the office or provide a separate room, try to find space for social areas where employees can relax, enjoy a bit of privacy, benefit from quiet time or social with their colleagues

64. THE COOL OFFICE EFFECT

Leading on from the previous point, the more funky, cool and stylish your office environment, the more great candidates are going to be beating a path to your door. Working in really plush or trendy offices has become a status symbol and it's something that your employees are likely to brag about to their friends.

While few businesses are in a position to commission the construction of a new, state-of-the-art company building, take a look at *officefurnitureexpress.co.uk/6-coolest-offices.htm* to see whether you can incorporate any of the ideas into your office environment to give it that real 'wow' factor.

It's not necessary to spend huge amounts of money doing this. Even simple things like changing the names of meeting rooms from dull old numbers to evocative names resonates with people.

Here's a few examples:

Facebook: Snuggle, ShakeWeight, Thighmaster (fitness product names)

Groupon: Unlimited Breadsticks, Tiny House for Big Ideas, This Used to Be a Forest

Instagram: Dragonstone, Dothraki Sea, Kings Landing, Riverrun (from the book 'Game of Thrones')

Buzzfeed: WTF, LOL, OMG, WIN

Remember, it's not just existing and potential employees who form an opinion of your business by the way it presents itself, but your clients and customers too. Shabby, run-down or old-fashioned premises speak of a company that's struggling or behind the times, so make sure that the physical environment that you provide doesn't give out the wrong message.

65. BUILD PRIVATE CALL AREAS

Like it or not, everyone needs to make personal calls during work hours from time to time. If employees feel that they can't do it openly then all that happens is that they'll use a company phone and pretend they're on a business call. Either that or they'll hide themselves away in the toilets or anywhere else where they're out of sight and probably take far longer on the call than if they'd been able to do it openly.

Providing employees with a couple of places where they can take their mobiles and have a conversation in private can bring about significant savings on company phone bills. If you go a step further and add a touch of cool by installing some of those old-fashioned red telephone boxes on your premises though, you can also reduce the amount of time they spend away from their desks on personal calls. Because they're in the phone box, everyone will know that they're on a personal call even if they can't hear the conversation, and that in itself is enough to encourage employees to keep it short!

66. DISHWASHERS ARE HEALTHIER

We all know how colds and flu can wipe out an office and leave employers short-staffed, but one of the easiest ways to cut down on the numbers of those nasty germs is simply by installing a dishwasher in the office kitchen.

Because dishwashers wash and dry at high temperatures, they're much more effective at killing off germs. The ease of stacking them also means that dirty dishes tend not to be left lying around for prolonged periods as is often the case when washing-up is done by hand.

Another great reason for investing in a dishwasher is that it avoids the scenario where the same person does the washing-up all of the time. Many of the gripes and groans that office colleagues have about one another revolve around issues like this and sometimes they can escalate if certain employees feel as though they are being disrespected or taken for granted.

67. SPARKLING BATHROOMS

Nothing speaks more of an employer's disregard for his workers than dirty or scruffy toilet facilities where the toilet paper always runs out before the end of the day. Clean, well-equipped facilities, on the other hand, not only give the message to employees and visitors that they're worth better, but also that your company expects a high standard in all things.

If possible, make sure that there is someone who is responsible for checking the state of the amenities at regular intervals during the day, and for replenishing stocks.

68. GREAT SMEL LING EMPLOYEES

Even if your business doesn't have its own on-site gym, you're never going to encourage your employees towards a healthier lifestyle if cycling to work or going for a run at lunchtime means having to spend the rest of the day looking, feeling and smelling bad.

Well-designed showers and changing rooms needn't take up huge amounts of space and they help to remove yet another one of the barriers that typically gets in the way of employees taking regular daily exercise. In addition, they're a huge bonus for employees who live at a distance from the office but want to go out straight after work.

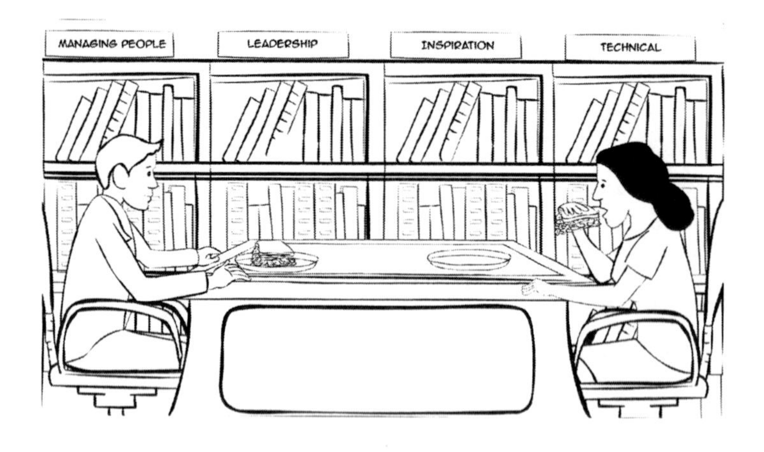
MANAGING PEOPLE
LEADERSHIP
INSPIRATION
TECHNICAL

PART 9
COMMUNICATING AND COACHING

For the many reasons that we've outlined in this book, employee reward and recognition schemes are absolutely crucial in being able to attract and retain exceptional employees. No matter how many treats and rewards a company provides, however, they still have no hope of achieving their aims if management processes are cumbersome and create additional work for employees, or if employees feel that their opportunities for career development are effectively impaired by outdated appraisal systems that limit visibility.

In this chapter, therefore, we're going to focus specifically on what your business can do to improve its approach to management and career development.

69. WHAT'S GOING ON

Nobody likes to be kept in the dark and in the workplace, as elsewhere, treating people like mushrooms is a guaranteed way to ensure that gossip, misinformation and mistrust prevail.

Whatever their role or wherever they are in the company hierarchy, employees aren't stupid.

They can see equally well when things are going well as when they are going badly. No matter how hard leaders and managers might try to hide a situation, the clues are always there! This makes it absolutely essential that openness, honesty and transparency are your company watchwords.

Good communication though, is also vital in terms of keeping employees up-to-date with news and changes within your organisation. After all, you can't expect them to input creative and innovative ideas if they don't know what's happening in the company as a whole. So, be sure to hold regular meetings where news of the company's financial performance can be shared, along with any other announcements that affect the business as a whole, or specific departments in particular. At *Clif Bar*, their weekly breakfast updates end with the 'consumer letter of the week', an idea which can act as a wonderful motivator to inspire employees to great things in the week to come.

70. YOU NEED AN 'EMERGENCY MEETING'

One of the key elements of employee motivation is trust, and what better opportunity to demonstrate faith in your employees' abilities than when you're away on holiday?

Actually, managers' holidays can be 'make or break time' when it comes to displaying trust, because if they don't feel 100% comfortable that things can be handled in their absence, there's that awful compulsion to keep phoning in. Not surprisingly, this makes employees feel as though they're being checked up on, not to mention destroying any opportunity they might otherwise have had to develop and learn through handling new experiences.

Next time you're due to take time away from the office on annual leave, take the opportunity to demonstrate your trust in your employee's by holding an 'emergency meeting'. Simply invite everyone along and brainstorm all the things that could possibly go wrong in your absence. Then, discuss and record what to do and who to contact in each situation. The resulting document then becomes your Emergency Plan.

Every business, and indeed every part of a business, should have its own Emergency and Business Continuity Plan anyway, so why not use a planned absence as an interesting way to create yours? The mere fact that your employee's have contributed to it will make them feel informed, trusted and empowered should something go wrong, and you, of course, will be able to relax and enjoy your holiday in the knowledge that everything is in good hands.

71. LESS ADMIN TIME? YES PLEASE

Especially for those employees whose primary work role isn't an administrative one, the amount of time spent writing reports can be hugely demoralising. Often they feel compelled to include the same issues over and over again because nothing ever gets done about them, and ultimately the hours spent writing reports that they suspect no-one will have time to read just feels like a whole lot of wasted effort.

Managers and leaders do need updates though, if they're going to gain a full appreciation of what's going on in the business – they just don't need them to turn into War and Peace! Why not scrap your current reporting system then, and try out the 15/5 method (sometimes called the 5/15 method) instead?

The whole idea behind 15/5 reporting is that it should take the writer no longer than 15 minutes to prepare, and the reader no longer than five minutes to read. Far from inhibiting communication, this simple system tends to have the opposite effect in that it keeps vital information flowing whilst at the same time making employees feel more comfortable about describing their goals and shouting about their successes. The very brevity of the report somehow makes people feel less self-conscious about sharing and celebrating their achievements.

For managers, 15/5 reports are a great way to keep their fingers on the pulse and they make it so much easier to spot problems and issues that need to be dealt with urgently. If you're looking for a product that will help you to keep track of what's going on within your team or department, then why not take a look at *iDoneThis.com*. Employees reply in the same succinct way as with a 15/5 report to a daily e-mail asking "What'd you get done today?" and the following morning a summary of everyone's accompishments is sent out to kick off the day.

72. KEEP PEOPLE ON THE SAME PAGE

Another useful online tool that you might want to consider is a task management tool which is provided by *Asana* (*asana.com*) and which is aimed at helping team members to stay on the same page. The shared task list lets team or project members plan, organise and stay in sync with one another. As well as putting tasks and conversations together so that users only have to go to one place to see the history of a piece of work, everyone involved can see who's doing what and what still needs to be done.

Of course, with so many team members working from different locations and even from home nowadays, Asana's task management tool can be an ideal solution for teams and managers who work remotely.

73. BITE SIZED CHUNKS

Most managers dread that annual review time of year. Alongside keeping up to date with their normal tasks and responsibilities, there's the additional job of gathering and presenting evidence relating to the performance of every one of their team members, and all before the deadline set by HR.

For employees too, the annual review process creates additional work and, unless they have been particularly conscientious about recording the various activities they've been involved in during the year, and their achievements, it can turn into an almost impossible memory test.

One of the biggest problems with the traditional approach to annual reviews is that there's simply too much information relating to too long a timescale, the consequence of which is that nothing other than the most recent activities feel relevant. This is clearly a problem identified by the creators of *Small Improvements*, a hosted SaaS software package which takes the pain out of annual reviews by focussing on smaller, shorter-term tasks and objectives and allowing users to combine:

1. Performance reviews
2. 360° feedback
3. Goals and objectives, and
4. Continuous feedback

thereby creating an ongoing picture of each individual's performance. Managers can even see at a glance how team members stack up against one another on an easy to use graph.

The real beauty of the *Small Improvements* system (*small-improvements.com*) is that it builds a continuous picture of employee performance. By the time the actual review comes around, all the necessary information is there and both employees and managers can make a more balanced appraisal of performance. In addition, employees have the satisfaction of feeling that they've had more of a say in the review process.

74. BE TOGETHER, BUT APART

Collaboration between team members is an essential part of business, but getting everyone together in the same place to do a progress check, decide on next steps and share ideas, plans and drawings that they're working on is not only expensive, but extremely time-consuming for everyone involved.

The traditional 'off-site' meeting came as a welcome excuse for employees to have a day away from the office, usually in a nice hotel at the company's expense. In today's workplace employees consider this outdated approach unnecessary; getting in the way of 'real' work and eating into their personal time. Not only is the technology available today to take meetings online but today's workers are comfortable and keen to use it.

Online conferencing facilities such as those offered by *GoToMeeting* and *join.me* are simple, easy-to-use web browser-based tools that not only provide audio and video conferencing, but also let users share what's on their computer screen with anyone who has access to the internet. Participants can join in from *PC*, *Mac*, *iPhone* or *Android* devices, making it possible for all employees to collaborate wherever they are. In the case of *Join.me*, there's a free app for up to 10 meeting participants which caters for internet calling, screen sharing, chat and sending files, but even if you upgrade to the pro version which provides a whole host of other functionality including a meeting scheduler, the cost is low and barely equates to the outlay for a single face-to-face meeting.

How you use online meeting facilities is really only limited by your imagination. *IBM*, for example, uses them to host 'lunch 'n' learn' sessions where employees have access to managers at all levels of the company. Instead of wasting time scratching around for information, they can get straight to the person who's 'in the know'. Their online 'innovation jamming sessions', meanwhile, provide a forum for employees around the world to share exciting new ideas.

75. SET UP AN INTERNAL SOCIAL NETWORK

Every business is an absolute mine of information, but sharing knowledge, especially when different teams and departments work remotely from one another, can be all but impossible. The result, of course, is that an endless amount of time is wasted as individuals seek solutions and answers independently and as delays occur in making crucial business decisions. By setting up a corporate social network, however, your company could provide easy access to the 'right' people at the 'right' time and more effectively pool its collective knowledge.

Corporate social networks, although in some ways similar to the likes of *Facebook* or *Twitter*, operate in a private environment which is for your employee's only. There's no need for privacy settings because everything that comes from within your organisation stays in your organisation. As with the more traditional social networks, however, they allow contact between people who might not otherwise have the opportunity to get together, whether for purely logistical reasons or because the individuals concerned work at entirely different levels within the company. Essentially they help to break down barriers in the pursuit of shared goals and objectives.

For employees, one of the enormous benefits of corporate social networks is that they help people to feel connected to their colleagues and co-workers. Often there's a sense of isolation when communication with people from other teams and departments takes place solely via e-mail or brief telephone conversations. As users can organise themselves into groups to tackle projects and meet common objectives, they offer the chance for everyone to feel involved and part of the team.

Another significant advantage for employees is that corporate social networks let them move outside their immediate job roles and into other areas of interest within the business. As well as giving them sight of the 'bigger picture', it allows them to develop their knowledge and progress within the company.

Because corporate social networks offer a less formal communication environment, workers typically find them an easier platform through which to express positive experiences and celebrate successes. Employees at *TD Canada Trust*, for example, use their unmoderated internal social network, Wow Moments, to share stories of positive customer experiences, and so successful has the network proved to be that 35,000 employees have generated 67,000 stories between them!

Glassboard (*glassboard.com*) and *Yammer* (*yammer.com*) are two private social networks which are widely used by businesses today, so why not check them out and get your business talking?

76. WALK AND TALK

The problem of how to bridge the divide between employees and leadership is one that exists in a great many of today's businesses. Even at the executive level, there's that feeling of needing to 'stand on ceremony' and a certain reluctance to share ideas or concerns with the company's chief. For those further down the ladder, meanwhile, the annual CEO visit typically takes the form of a generic, pre-prepared speech which is invariably followed by a whole lot of awkward silence. Far from helping to bridge the gap, these forced, impersonal events often have the effect of widening it further.

In many ways, it's quite understandable that CEO's 'walkabouts' often fall flat on their faces. After all, most people simply aren't brave enough to voice their ideas and opinions in front of a large audience – especially one that includes their line manager and the head of the company. Unfortunately for the business though, this can make it hard to get rid of that 'them and us' divide, whilst at the same time leaving leaders unable to tap into the ideas and experience of their workers and the workers feeling as though they have no voice.

Perhaps it was because of some of these issues that the CEO of *Answerlab* decided to take a different approach by introducing the CEO Walk and Talk. Rather than addressing the company as a whole or in larger groups, the company's leader literally takes each employee out of the office for an hour-long walk, during which the individual has the opportunity to share any concerns or ideas directly.

The idea works well, not only because the interaction is at a much more personal level, but also because being away from the formal office environment makes workers more comfortable and relaxed enough to participate fully.

Of course, whilst the CEO Walk and Talk might be viable within companies with lower numbers of employees, it simply isn't possible to spend one-to-one time with hundreds or even thousands of employees. Even in these cases though, there's nothing to stop you from following the example of *Apple's* Steve Jobs by using this tactic to discuss, develop and share ideas with your executive team.

77. INTERN INCUBATOR

Internships don't just offer the perfect chance for students and recent graduates to gain much-needed on-the-job experience; for employers they represent ideal opportunities to select from, and 'test drive' some of the industry's best new talent.

To really get the best out of your intern programme, try moving interns and those on work placements around each department rather than assigning them to one particular area, and always let them shadow the very best people that the department has to offer. Throughout the programme, set them tasks, both individually and as part of a team, and then at the end, ask each one to present three suggestions that will either improve your existing business or bring about greater business opportunity.

One of the key reasons for approaching intern programmes in this way lies in the fact that a fresh pair of eyes and an 'innocent' mind can often spot fairly obvious opportunities that are missed by more experienced employees. Once people have been in the job for a while, it becomes more difficult to see the wood for the trees! In addition though, the process will help you to identify potential new recruits for the future.

If the length of your programme permits, another great idea is to use one of your interns as the manager of a project team. Choose a project which has been on your 'nice to do when we have time' list, such as a research project, the rewriting of an outdated document or the creation of training materials, and then provide them with the resources to set up, develop and run the project away from the eyes and ears of their current peers. At the same time as helping to develop an aspiring manager, this will foster an environment in which they can try things out and experiment without the fear of failing in front of their colleagues and co-workers.

To help further with this process, you could also support them with a mentor for the project. Ideally, this individual would be from a different department and would be someone who understands that their role is to help with the development of the project manager, rather than to control the project.

78. EXPENSES APPS

One of the biggest frustrations for managers is that they often get so bogged down in administrative tasks that they don't actually have time to manage. Given the salaries that managers typically expect, this is clearly a huge frustration for business leaders too. With a simple solution such as an expenses app your business could alleviate some of the administrative burden, leaving managers to get on with the tasks that truly make use of their skills and talents.

Products such as *Expensify* (*expensify.com*) and Recipt Bank (*receipt-bank.com*) provide a ready-made solution to the job of managing expenses. With free mobile apps on all platforms and a system which integrates with the major online payroll or accounting package, *Expensify* takes the pain out of expense management by allowing employees to capture receipts and submit expense claims anywhere.

Another option, however, is to build your own expenses app. For less than £10k, you could build an app that lets employees photograph their receipts, verify the information and choose the appropriate expenses categories before automatically submitting it to the relevant manager. At the end of each week, the manager receives a summary to the app on his phone which he can either sign off at a higher level or use as the basis to drill right down to receipt level if he so chooses.

While introducing an off-the-shelf expenses app will still save everyone in the process a lot of time and highlight your organisation's commitment to improving business processes, one of the great benefits of developing your own app is that you could even generate another revenue stream by selling the technology to other companies once you have it up and running perfectly.

79. JOURNEY PLANNER APP

Another useful app that might be worth considering is a journey planner app which registers employees' journey plans and pushes the information through to their line manager. Usually, of course, this information has to be submitted manually in support of mileage claims, but as with expense management, manual systems tend to be hugely onerous and time-consuming.

Another benefit of using a journey planner app is that it can provide tremendously useful management information. Used as a reporting tool, it could capture and report information such as the length and regularity of visits, thereby freeing managers up to deal with the consequences of the report findings rather than bogging them down in producing the report in the first place.

80. EYE CONTACT RULES

We've all felt the frustration of trying to have a conversation with someone who seems more intent on looking at their computer screen or picking up texts on their mobile phone. Even in our personal lives this behaviour tends to leave us feeling that we're not really being listened to or that we're somehow 'in the way'. In the workplace though, the effects can amount to more than just mild irritation.

When managers fail to give their full and undivided attention to their employee's, the message that they communicate is that the input of the employee is less important than the other task that they're trying to focus on. Even if it only happens once, the employee is, quite understandably, left feeling demoralised and wondering "Why do I even bother?". If it happens consistently though, that sense of demoralisation can quickly turn into a total lack of confidence in the manager and, even, outright mistrust.

The key way that any of us can tell if a listener is fully engaged in what we have to say is whether or not they give us full eye to eye contact. Clearly if someone is busy checking their computer screen or *iPhone*, then this isn't the case. Make it a rule in your organisation, therefore, that when managers are talking to their employee's, mobile phones should be put on one side and computer screens locked unless the information on them needs to be shared as part of the conversation.

Another thing that's worth remembering is that truly listening to employees isn't just about showing basic courtesy. Every member of the team has an input to make and if managers don't pay full attention then important information can be missed and wrong decisions made as a result.

81. START A 'CATCH PEOPLE DOING IT RIGHT' CULTURE

The daily challenges of working life can often make it much easier for everyone to focus on the negatives rather than the positives. Once this starts to happen, it's only a short spiral down into demotivation and disengagement. By creating a 'catch people doing it right' culture, however, it's entirely possible to nip negativity in the bud and give great employees the recognition they deserve.

Try making it a requirement of senior managers to bring to their regular monthly or quarterly meetings the best example of something that one of their team members has done really well. Don't just stop there though; instead, oblige somebody else at the meeting to praise the individual or, at the very least, to simply go and talk to them about the particular contribution they have made to their team.

Creating a culture of positivity in this way not only ensures that exceptional employees experience the feel-good factor that comes with being appropriately recognised for their work. It also has the added benefit of fostering a wider appreciation of the challenges faced by different teams and departments across the organisation and of their successes and achievements.

82. INVEST IN POSITIVE FEEDBACK

Every manager has to face the situation where a team member has either failed to live up to expectations or even made an outright blunder from time to time. How those situations are handled though, can make all the difference between whether the employee walks away feeling demoralised or treats it as a learning experience and moves on.

Whilst it is, of course, important for managers to get their message across and avoid the repetition of undesirable actions or behaviours, that message will be much more readily accepted if the bitter pill is sugar coated. Remember the words of Mary Poppins: "just a spoonful of sugar helps the medicine go down".

When it comes to sharing constructive criticism, one of the most commonly-used and effective approaches involves communicating three positive comments before tackling anything that criticises an individual's performance. The 'before' part is important because whilst there are those who believe in 'sandwiching' the criticism between two points of praise, often this has the effect of devaluing the praise to the extent that the recipient only hears the criticism.

Sharing constructive criticism is an important art in the business world, although not necessarily one that is mastered by all managers. While many companies invest huge amounts of money in different types of management training, often these fail to address the issue of how to give feedback in a positive way that will encourage rather than demotivate employees. Whether you employ internal or external training providers, therefore, always ensure that the courses they deliver equip your managers with this vital skill.

Oh, and another extremely important point... always encourage your managers to give constructive criticism in private. Nothing is more demoralising and embarrassing for employees than being criticised in front of their peers, and nothing is more damaging to your business than to have it happen in front of your clients or customers!

83. LUNCHTIME LESSONS

While formal training and on-the-job learning are both incredibly important in terms of equipping workers with the necessary skills and knowledge to carry out their duties and providing them with development opportunities, both of course tend to focus primarily on the individual's direct job role. Many people, however, would jump at the chance to broaden their knowledge to encompass different areas of the business or to deepen it in their own specialist field. One great way to provide them with this opportunity is by creating a voluntary learning forum within your workplace. U.S healthcare company *Patients Like Me* holds educational lunches every week which are available to all employees.

Now, although your business might choose to bear the expense of hiring specialist speakers to host 'turn up and learn' sessions, in most cases the expertise that employees are seeking is already in the business. Simply arrange your sessions to take place, for example over lunch on a Friday, and get one of your own senior specialists to present on a specific topic and provide help and advice with particular problems or tasks that employees are dealing with in their work lives. Make these voluntary sessions informal so that workers can eat while they're listening and either participate actively or take more of a back seat.

Aside from the fact that using your own senior experts to host voluntary learning forums won't cost your business anything, another great advantage is that they can speak directly to what your organisation does and the way it works. This, of course, makes the learning experience far more relevant than if the same subject were to be addressed by an outsider.

84. FREE OFFICE LIBRARY

Earlieroninthisbook,wetalkedaboutencouraging reading by providing every employee with a free *Kindle* and a monthly allowance to be spent on book downloads of their choice. Alongside or as an alternative to this initiative, however, another great idea is to provide a free office library that all of your employee's can make use of.

Although, as we mentioned previously, any kind of book can be deemed to be educational in some respect, one of the key benefits of setting up your own library is that you can stock it with reading matter which is relevant to your business. That doesn't mean to say that you need only include technical manuals of course. Instead, you can also invest in the best business, inspirational and personal development books that you can find and make these readily available for any employee to borrow.

Just to come back to technical manuals, these are of course a very welcome addition to any business library and can act as a reliable source of reference, provided that they are up to date. As many such books tend to be a little on the expensive side though, often they can be out of the reach of individual employees, so including them in your library stock will make them available to everyone.

85. START A MENTORING PROGRAM

Setting up a mentoring programme is one of the single most powerful things a business can do, for itself, its newly-promoted managers and its most exceptional workers in particular. *Burton Snowboards* even has a dedicated leadership program for the women in their management team. For everyone's benefit, programmes tend to work best if the person chosen as the mentor isn't the employee's own line manager or even someone who is in their chain of line management, but rather another senior individual from a different area of the business. You'll see why this is the case in just a moment.

As can be seen from the following list of benefits, some of the greatest advantages of setting up a mentoring programme lie in the areas of recruitment, retention and succession planning:

- The promise of a structured mentoring programme and a supportive mentor is hugely attractive to the most talented and motivated job candidates, so employers who can offer this get the pick of the crop
- Employees who take part in mentoring programmes tend to stay with their employers because they feel more engaged, can see a clear path mapped out in front of them and know that their company is working with them to achieve their goals and ambitions

- Because mentored employees don't just receive advice and guidance in relation to their direct job role but also development in areas such as leadership, self-awareness, teamwork and compromise. Not only do they become more effective more quickly within the organisation, but they also acquire the skills to take over senior roles and as such form a crucial part of a business' succession planning strategy.

In addition, mentoring programmes offer:

- A safe and confidential environment in which the mentored employee can learn and discuss issues without being judged
- A sounding board for the mentored employee ideas
- An opportunity for the individual to get to grips more quickly and thoroughly with the company's culture
- The chance for both parties to learn about their respective areas of the business and transfer knowledge
- The opportunity to foster strong relationships between two areas of the business, which can be especially useful if they need to work collaboratively

If your business is considering setting up its own mentoring programme, there are a few factors which are worth bearing in mind to make it truly successful:

- Make sure that the mentor is provided with training in coaching and mentoring skills as bad mentoring can have hugely demotivational effects
- Try to give the mentoring process some context or objective. You might, for example, focus on helping the mentored employee to improve his or her skills in three specific areas or to work on specific relationships within the business
- Trust between both parties is absolutely essential for the relationship to work, so always ensure that your company mentors do not abuse the relationship politically or act in any way that might undermine the individual

86. NEW THINKING SESSIONS

When we think of a mentoring programme, what invariably comes to mind is a situation where a more senior and experienced employee takes a more junior employee under their wing. In some areas, however, it is the incoming 'juniors' who have the edge over longer-term employees when it comes to experience.

One perfect example of this is in the area of technology. Even someone entirely new to the workplace who been brought up in the technological age could have exceptional skills that can be shared. Not only is this incredibly beneficial to the company as a whole, but the junior employees themselves gain confidence more quickly and have the satisfaction of being able to share their knowledge.

Another area where more junior employees can contribute greatly to the process of teaching and learning is in relation to the recent training courses that they have attended. In all areas of business, things change and methods become outdated. If any of your newer employees have studied or learned about new methods, either before joining your company or as part of their initial training, then give them the chance to spread the word.

One of the reasons that longer-serving employees can sometimes fall behind the times is simply because they work alongside the same colleagues day in, day out, and nobody has anything new to input. So that everyone gets the benefit of the great new things that junior employees have to offer, why not look for ways to make it easier for employees to swap shifts and communicate more easily?

87. 1 in 3 EFFICIENCY

As we mentioned a little earlier, one of the key challenges of managing groups of employees who spend much of their time on the road lies in the time and effort expended on checking their travel and expenses claims. Managers who check every last entry on every claim form can find themselves filling entire days with what is essentially an administrative task, and that's really not something that any business can afford. By using the 1 in 3 method though, the time taken to verify expense claims can literally be cut to one third.

One of the main reasons why so many managers feel obliged to go through the laborious process of checking expense forms line by line is because if they don't do a thorough check and their employee's pick up on this, they'll leave themselves exposed to inaccuracies and possibly even to fraud. The trick then, is to make employees think that you're checking everything when in fact you're not. Here's how it works...

When a new employee joins the team, check their expense claims thoroughly, line by line, for the first three months. If you find an error or inconsistency, send the form back to the employee unsigned and get them to correct it before signing it off. Even if you don't find anything wrong still make a point of querying something, such as who they bought coffee or lunch for, so that the claimant knows that you have given the claim your full attention. Soon, this level of vigilance will pay off and the accuracy level of the claims submitted will rise.

After a period of three months during which the employee has submitted perfect claims, you can now start checking just one claim in three thoroughly. The employee will still be expecting you to check every single line and to reject any claims containing errors, so by this time he or she will effectively be policing their own work, which means you don't have to. Of course, if you do happen to find any problems or mistakes with the one that you check, you can always go back to the previous two months and give these the once-over if you think that would be appropriate.

Provided you query any errors that you come across in the claims that you check thoroughly, you'll still keep the employee on their toes and they'll be unlikely to make further mistakes. In the meantime though, you will have succeeded in reducing your own burden to a third of what it was originally, and the only small trade-off is that if you do find a problem, you might have to do a retrospective check of two months at worst.

88. CREATE A RECRUITMENT REFERRAL ENGINE

Employee referral bonus schemes are relatively common within today's businesses, but while some work very effectively in terms of getting new people on board, often they do little to help with employees retention. Even though employers might save on the initial hiring costs, when employees leave, they still forfeit the training costs and suffer the inevitable drop in revenue that comes with getting new workers up to speed. By adding a twist to employee referral schemes though, existing workers can be given greater incentive to focus more on the quality of the candidates that they put forward, as well as on encouraging them to stay within the business for longer.

The *Chipotle* chain of Mexican restaurants focuses its managers on hiring potential future managers for entry-level roles by offering rewards based on how long new employees stay with the company, whether they get promoted and, if so, to what level. Existing employees don't just have the opportunity to receive one reward though, but can earn additional bonuses as their referees move higher up the ladder or stay on longer.

So, based on *Chipotle's* scheme, you might, for example, give someone a bonus of £1,000 if they refer someone who then stays on for three years. If that same individual is still with you two years' later, however, you would then reward the referring manager with a further £1,000.

Following the same principle, if one of your managers refers someone who is subsequently promoted to the position of supervisor, the referring manager would receive a bonus of £2,500. If the supervisor then goes on to become a manager, then the original manager would receive a further £5,000, and if they make it to senior manager level, the reward would be a whopping £10,000!

This scheme proved so successful for *Chipotle* that they reported in 2011 that 97% of their restaurant managers were people who had been promoted from hourly-paid positions into the business!

As you might imagine, for a scheme like this to work well, the rewards on offer must be worth having. If the examples given seem excessive though, then just think about how much a business with a traditionally high turnover of employees would have spent on recruitment and training within the same period of time.

You can of course adapt the system that we've described here to incentivise any hiring manager. Although you might need to decide on a different set of rewards, if you use the scheme to focus them on hiring the right people and ensure that they are invested in developing their teams in the right way, then the results could be equally impressive as those achieved by *Chipotle*.

WELCOME

PART 10
RECRUITMENT WOWS

Most of the tips for rewarding, recognising and engaging people that we've looked at so far have been focused on existing employees. Even if you follow these but your recruitment process is in any way shoddy all your good work is ultimately going to be undone. In this chapter, we're going to look at some of the things that you can do to stand out as an ace recruiter.

89. WRITE AWESOME VACANCY ADVERTS

It might be an employer's market out there at the moment but believe me, hiring the very best employees is never a one-way street. As much as you're judging and evaluating your job applicants, those talented and committed potential candidates are also evaluating your company.

In most cases, the first impression that potential candidates have of your business is through your job advertisements. While this might not seem like a big deal, if your ads:

- Are either short on detail or long-winded and irrelevant
- Are full of grammatical or spelling errors
- Aren't laid out clearly
- Don't make the role or your company sound appealing, or
- Fail to make it clear how the applicant should respond

then you simply won't attract high calibre candidates. After all, if that's the best you can do with a job advert, what would you be like to work for?

A job advertisement is just like any other ad. Its aim is to sell. You wouldn't expect your customers or clients to buy your product or service based on a second-rate ad, so don't expect great candidates to buy into your company on that basis either.

90. FOLLOW UP ALL APPLICATIONS

Again, perhaps because it has been, over recent years, an employer's market and because many companies are finding themselves inundated with job applications, but many seem to be using this as an excuse for not responding to potential candidates. This, however, is an oversight because:

1. It's not a great reflection on your business generally and can easily create negative PR. It's easy to think that nobody will know if you don't bother to acknowledge your job applicants, but you'd be amazed at how quickly word travels and how keen people are to vote with their feet if they come across something they don't like.
2. It's lazy bad manners and is disrespectful to potential candidates who have paid you the compliment of demonstrating that they'd like to work for your business

Before you even post a job advertisement, decide on how you're going to let your applicants know whether they're in or out of the running. Automated response systems aren't great, but in many cases they are necessary when businesses have thousands of applications to deal with. Whether you choose a manual or an automated system though, always make sure that you do respond to each and every individual who applies.

91. REJECT QUICKLY AND FAIRLY

These are two more traps that many businesses fall into. In some cases they delay in telling applicants that they haven't been successful for weeks or even months, and in the vast majority of cases applicants never discover why they were counted out of the running. Again though, there are good reasons why your business needs to behave differently if it's going to stay ahead of the competition.

When it comes to response times, it's really back to basic courtesy. You wouldn't expect an applicant to take weeks to get back to you, so don't imagine that they're going to feel any different. Even if it's bad news, candidates would rather know so that they can act accordingly. Leaving them hanging reflects badly on your business.

In the case of candidates whom you have interviewed, it is always vital to let them know without delay that they've been unsuccessful and why. After all, if these individuals were of a high enough calibre that you chose to interview them in the first place, then who's to say that you might not want to hire them at some time in the future?

92. KEEP THE 'NO'S' IN THE FAMILY

Often when businesses have been through the interview process it's a very close call between two or more good candidates. In these cases, it pays the company to leave the door open in case another suitable position arises and to treat the unsuccessful candidates like they're 'part of the family' even though they have been turned down on this occasion.

One way to do this is to reward them for their great performance in the same way as you would with your current employee's. You might, for example, send them to a discount voucher to use on your goods or services by way of a thank you. Not only will this make your business really stand out, but it will give the candidates a great insight into your culture and how you treat your employees so that they'll still be keen to join you at a later stage.

93. PAY THE UNCOMMITED TO LEAVE

Given that employees who are entirely committed to your business are such a huge asset, it makes sense to be able to sort out precisely who is committed and who isn't at the earliest possible opportunity.

At *Zappos*, the online retailer that uses peer-to-peer bonus systems as one of its reward and recognition schemes, they use a tactic that's guaranteed to sort out the wheat from the chaff. After training their new recruits for two weeks on full pay, they then offer them $2,000 (approx £1,250) as an inducement to leave. It's a great reflection on the company that almost everyone refuses the offer, but theirs is certainly an innovative and cost-effective way of finding out who's committed to the organisation!

94. MAKE THE FIRST DAY A WOW

The first day in a new job can be nerve-wracking time for most people, and not too unlike the first day of school. The main difference is that nursery teachers tend to go out of their way to make every new class of children feel comfortable and welcome. They show them where to hang up their coats, and given a tour of the school. Once they're in the classroom, all the resources they need to start their days are ready and waiting for them. Those first few days though, typically don't see them being thrown in at the deep end. Teachers ease young students in gradually so as not to overwhelm them and help them realise that school isn't such a bad place to be after all.

Now of course your new employees aren't children, but actually many of the fears and emotions that they feel on their first day are not so dissimilar to the ones they experienced when they were four or five years old. Unlike their younger selves, however, new employees are typically trying to make a great first impression on top of everything else!

What about the employers though? Not that many work hard, like the nursery teachers, to make that first day a welcoming experience. Often they're not even there on the first day, and even if they are, they palm them off on some poor junior employee who doesn't really know what to do with them and may even have applied for the job themselves.

Welcome to the company!

The tone that you set on an employee's first day will make a lasting impression throughout their time with your company. It will impact on their confidence (in themselves and your business) and on whether they feel valued by the organisation, and it will give them an early insight into how they can expect to be treated by your business. Ultimately, of course, it will also reflect on their relationships with their managers, their co-workers and their customers and clients too.

So, what can employers, and the managers of new employees in particular, do to really wow them right from the word go? Here are a few great ideas which are sure to make them want to keep coming back for more.

- Make the first day a slightly later start than normal so that your new employee doesn't arrive feeling flustered if they hit traffic problems or can't find anywhere to park, and so that everyone can prepare for their arrival. Some businesses find it better to start new people on a Friday when things are quieter and everyone has more time to welcome new starters on board
- Don't leave new employees to find their own way from the entrance to the building to the office. Be there waiting to greet them at the door
- Give them a proper welcome and let them know how pleased the company is to have them on board

- Arrange for someone on reception to take their coat and make them a drink
- Show the new employees member to their desk, but make sure beforehand that all the resources and supplies they could possibly need have been provided. For that really special touch, pre-record their name on their voicemail message to make them feel like 'part of the family' right from the start. You could even put up a 'Welcome' banner with the individual's name on it too
- Make sure that their business cards are printed in advance and waiting for them on their desk. Again, for that real 'wow' factor, get all the team members to sign a backing card with a welcome message and frame it alongside one of the newcomer's business cards
- Give them 10 minutes or so to get settled before meeting with the boss for an informal welcome chat. Also, share a bit about the company's history, how it got to where it is today and how your new employee is now part of that history. Be sure to include anything that's unique about your organisation and that your new hire wouldn't necessarily know
- Give them a guided tour of the building, being careful to point out restrooms and other employee facilities on the way. Introduce them to people as you go, but make sure that everyone knows their name, job title and a little bit about them

in advance. Follow the tour with lunch but don't be tempted to invite the whole of the team to join you at this stage. There's little more embarrassing than trying to make conversation with a new group of people when you've got a mouth full of food

- Use the period directly after lunch to get your new employee to fill in just the most essential paperwork and forms, with the rest being completed throughout the course of the week. Also, talk them through any benefits, insurances and so on that they can expect to receive and any other important HR-related information
- Team them up for the rest of the afternoon with each of their new colleagues for a one-to-one introduction. This will give them the opportunity to get to know a little about one another, as well as for your new employee to learn something about the other roles in the team
- When it gets to the end of the first day, the new employee's boss presents them with a wrapped gift, not for the employee but for his or her 'significant other'. The gift should be accompanied by a card expressing the company's thanks for helping the new employee to make the decision to join them

Businesses that really go out of their way to make new employees' first days special are few and far between. Making that extra effort though, could not only ensure that your company stands out from the competition, but also that all of your new employee's are committed to your business for the long run. Massachusetts removals company *Gentle Giant* has an unusual initiation 'welcome' for all new employees - they hold a race with Peter O'Toole, the CEO, and any other employee who wants to welcome the new starter up and down the stadium seating at the nearby Harvard Stadium. In total they run up 1,000 steps - a genuine physical challenge, which is followed by breakfast and an orientation speech from the CEO. This rite came about after O'Toole initiated the run as a way to emphasise to employees he wants them to push themselves and to show that he will continue to do so too. Many employees come back and try to improve their time and to show support for those who are doing it for the first time.

95. GIVE THEM THE BEST POSSIBLE START

Whenever new employees join an organisation there is a tremendous drive to learn about the company, to fit in quickly with the business culture and to fully get to grips with what's expected of them. A wise employer capitalises on this initial enthusiasm and uses it during the early days to ensure a seamless and fast induction to the company.

The founder and executive team of *Zulily*, an online retailer of top quality clothes and accessories for mothers, babies and children, take the opportunity each month to spend time with groups of employees who have recently joined the business. The focus of these hour-long sessions is the history and culture of the business, and the main reason for holding them is to ensure that new starters quickly become acclimatised to their new and fast-changing environments and therefore become more effective in their roles at an earlier stage.

Zulily's leadership team don't just stop there though. At each of their new recruits' one month, two month and three month anniversaries, they meet with the same groups of people to gather their feedback on their experience with the company to date. Essentially this acts as a temperature check to see how well their new employees are settling in, something which is especially important in an organisation which is growing so quickly.

If you're looking for a more unusual way to help your new hires to become acclimatised to your business, then you might want to consider one of the web-based services that use social networking and games to inject a bit of fun into the process. *AllAboard* software (by *MindTickle*) sends an introductory e-mail to new hires directing them to a personalised greetings page and lots of fun trivia games that focus on the company's history, culture and product offering, *AllAboard* helps them to learn about their organisation from videos and slideshows and then lets them win prizes by answering trivia questions.

96. GIFT FOR THE OFFICE

Everyone likes receiving gifts, so what better way to help your latest recruits to break the ice with their new colleagues than by giving them a budget to buy a gift for the office when they join?

London advertising agency *St Luke's* uses this tactic for its new starters. It gives £150 to each of them and simply asks that they buy something for everyone. The tactic works well because not only does it encourage the giver to find out a bit about the people he or she is buying for, but the choice of gifts often gives the recipient a pretty good insight into the new employee.

97. UTILISE EXISTING BRAINS AND EXPERIENCE

Let's face it, company inductions can often be quite dry affairs, especially when messages about the organisation's heritage, values and vision are delivered by someone in HR or a starter's new manager who has probably given the same spiel endless times before. Handing over part of the induction process to longer-serving employees and peers who are less likely to be seen as just 'toeing the party line', on the other hand, can not only make the messages sound more genuine and heartfelt, but also has the added benefit of helping to reaffirm the speakers' own belief in the company and enthusiasm for what it stands for.

Rather than just having existing employees stand up and say their piece at induction sessions, a great idea is to turn excerpts from these sessions into a video that you could use as a marketing tool for candidates that you intend to interview. As we have already mentioned, there's something about learning about an organisation from the workers 'at the coal face' that makes it far more compelling and believable than if the same messages were delivered by, for example, a member of the leadership or HR team.

98. HAVE A NEW STARTER BUDDY SYSTEM

Every business has its own unique culture and way of doing things, and clearly the more quickly and easily new starters become accustomed to these, the better for everyone concerned. Setting up a 'buddy' system is a really effective way to help new starters settle in and get off to a flying start.

A 'buddy', in this sense, is basically someone who partners with a new employee during their early days in the company. Their role is to create a welcoming environment, to offer support and guidance, to share experiences that will help the new recruit to acclimatise easily and to quickly allow them to become effective in terms of their role and responsibilities. Buddy systems, meanwhile, encourage the sharing of knowledge and feedback, as well as assisting with the development of new perspectives and working practices.

Although perhaps the more obvious choice of buddy for a new starter might be someone from within their own team, actually the most successful pairings are those with someone from a different department who, ideally, has connections with the same people within the organisation. One of the main reasons for this is because it removes any feeling on the part of the new hire of being judged by his or her peers or any sense of competition between the pair. If the new recruit needs to ask the same question a dozen times, for example, they are likely to feel less embarrassed about doing so with someone who is not a direct co-worker.

Acting as a buddy isn't something that should be taken lightly by employees. The role comes with its own level of responsibility and, as such, it can be a good idea to incentivise your buddies to do a great job with a reward or bonus which is related to the performance of the new starter.

99. GIVE OUTSIDERS A TASTE

The reality is that most workplaces these days continue to be dull, uninspiring and not that great. Which is why - once you have a great environment and culture in place - you must give potential employees a chance to sample it.

Chicago based software firm *37 Signals* (whose *Basecamp* software is perfect for the small business community) have a great way of making this happen: they offer their private mini-theatre free to local small businesses who want to put events, whether training or sales. This means that most weeks the local small business community is bringing their customers and employees in direct contact with the culture and environment that *37 Signals* have created (and is generally regarded as awesome). No wonder that they have no problem attracting the best talent and often all they do is post an ad on the blog area of their own website!

LET'S MAKE A START

Throughout this book we have outlined dozens of imaginative ways to reward and recognise employees at all stages of their careers, as well as to encourage and motivate them to try even harder to make the businesses they work in more successful. Before rushing off to put these ideas into action, it's worth remembering that there are both right and wrong ways of getting started.

Even the most potentially motivating and engaging initiatives can fall flat on their faces if an organisation isn't totally committed to a culture of genuine appreciation. People are generally smart enough to see right through schemes that do nothing more than pay lip service to the principles of employee engagement. The trouble is though, that not only do badly implemented schemes fail to have the desired effect, they actually end up making employees feel even more unappreciated and demotivated than they were in the first place!

There are countless cringeworthy examples of employers making misguided efforts to engage their workers and boost morale. Take, for instance, the company that 'generously' decided to donate its employee's Christmas bonuses to charity. Not only were its employees deprived of a reward that most would have found useful during the festive period, but the CEO actually had the gall to use the initiative as a publicity stunt by hiring a photographer to take pictures of him holding a huge novelty cheque at the

Christmas lunch! Then there was the manager who hired a clown to help alleviate the stress of workers who were giving their all to a big, new project. You can just imagine the reaction of these tense, serious, exhausted people to an entertainer whose fooling around only disrupted their work and whose mere presence suggested that they could be cajoled like children, into a better frame of mind.

Engagement initiatives that come across in any way as being condescending or disingenuous are doomed from the start. Even the ideas that we have outlined in this book, however, will fail to hit the spot if the middle managers responsible for rewarding and recognising employees don't have the right attitudes or skills. Managers who themselves are disengaged, for example, or those who are perceived by their workers as bullies, don't stand a chance of being able to choose the right initiatives for a particular group of employees or of introducing them without suspicion of an ulterior motive. You need to start, therefore, by making sure that the middle managers in your organisation are fully on board with the concepts of creating a culture of appreciation, and that they have the necessary skills and resources available to them to do just that. Once these issues have been addressed, here are a few more ideas of how to get started the right way:

1. **Don't try to fix a problem that doesn't exist**

   It's easy to imagine that all businesses suffer with the problem of disengaged workers. Making a big deal about raising levels of motivation when employees are quite happy as they are, can actually make them feel less, rather than more engaged. While it almost certainly wouldn't hurt to introduce a few more thoughtful reward and recognition schemes in these cases, forcing employees to focus on non existent negatives that aren't really there will only cause their levels of motivation to spiral downwards.

2. **Be sure to get to the root of the real problem**

   If general levels of engagement and morale are low within your organisation, no amount of free lunches is going to get things back on track. The feelings of demotivation that afflict most businesses don't spring up overnight and they won't respond to a quick fix either. When starting on the road to creating a great new organisational culture, always be sure to identify and deal with the real root of the problem before offering 'nice to have' initiatives and incentives.

3. **Be careful how you introduce new ideas**

   In businesses where levels of employee engagement are already low, employees can be quite sceptical of new initiatives which are ultimately designed to bring benefit to the employer. Take care, both in terms of how you introduce new ideas within your organisation and the type of initiatives that you introduce in order to maintain credibility.

4. **Use key employees as feedback loops**

   In every business there are people who are trusted and whose opinions are valued highly by other members of employees. Rather than relying entirely on managers whose motives may be questioned by employees, use these 'influencers' as feedback loops to gauge the engagement 'temperature' within your organisation, get to the real roots of any issues and introduce new ideas. Not only will this help the business in its bid to introduce a new culture, but it compliments the influencers into the bargain.

5. **Recognise the 'behind the scenes' people who keep the business going**

   Although we've talked about recognising and rewarding employees who excel in their everyday roles or in the execution of special projects, it's important not to forget those who work behind the scenes to keep the business going. Be sure to acknowledge those individuals who inspire others with their positivity, for example, by creating special awards.

6. **Sort out basic benefits first**

   Many companies offer a range of more traditional benefits to their employees, such as:

- Paid holidays in excess of the legal minimum
- Private healthcare, dental, disability and life insurances
- Interest-free loans for travel season tickets
- Incentives to reduce the number of employees who travel to work by car, such as the cycle to work scheme in the UK which offers discounts on bicycles for employees
- Discounts on company products or services

These benefits have quite deliberately been omitted from this book because of course most employers are already aware of them. If, however, any of these don't form part of the remuneration packages that you offer to your workers, then do consider introducing them first before looking at more creative benefits such as airport lounge cards. Remember, the reason why the benefits listed above are more commonly offered is because they are some of the most valuable to employees.

GIVE THEM BELIEF

In his book entitled 'Drive – The Surprising Truth About What Motivates Us', world-renowned business writer, Dan Pink, talks about the limitations of the 'carrot and stick' approach to improving levels of motivation amongst today's generation of workers. As he explains, rewarding the types of behaviour that employers want to encourage whilst 'punishing' those that they want to discourage might work in some circumstances, but it does nothing to motivate individuals in the direction of the kind of creative and conceptual thought that helps businesses to grow and prosper.

Countless research studies indicate that today's employees want mastery, appreciation and self-direction. Those employers who ensure that these vital elements are present within the workplace are rewarded with contented, engaged and loyal employees, while those who don't pay the price, both financially and otherwise.

What precisely do we mean by mastery, appreciation and self-direction though?

- Mastery is about learning and building on our skills. As the word suggests, it's about mastering or becoming expert at the things we choose to do, and it's something that many consider to be an innate need that resides within all of us. After all, most of us spend our valuable leisure time applying ourselves to mastering subjects and interests without there being any financial reward for our efforts.

- Appreciation, once again, is something that we human beings don't just want, but seem to need in our lives if we are to continue feeling motivated. Sometimes all that's needed to spur us on is a pat on the back, and indeed when it comes to financial rewards, provided the level of reward is sufficient to take the question of money off the table, anything more can actually have a detrimental impact on performance. As we have described in this book there are numerous ways for employers to show appreciation which cost little or nothing.
- Self-direction is something which has been highlighted as being especially relevant to Generation Y and Millennial workers. Unlike some previous generations of employees who thrived on being given close direction from their managers and bosses, today's younger workers want to be able to decide for themselves how to go about achieving an objective and then be left alone to get on with it.

As we mentioned earlier, meeting the needs of today's workers isn't about pandering needlessly to the desires of a bunch of spoilt youngsters who think the world owes them a living. The world is a changed place and people's priorities and concerns are, quite understandably, very different in the twenty-first century, getting the best of out todays workforce involves adopting an entirely new approach that takes into account a changed, but equally valid view of what matters, and for employers that means doing five key things:

1. Giving them belief - showing that you believe in your workers as individuals and in their capabilities
2. Showing them trust - demonstrating that you have faith in their abilities and then giving them the freedom to take the lead in achieving their objectives
3. Being clear on objectives - giving them a clear foundation on which to build by letting them know exactly what results you expect, rather than setting them up to fail
4. Celebrating in public - recognising their successes and achievements and helping them to share their glory and motivate others
5. Correcting in private - allowing them the opportunity to learn from their mistakes without suffering any shame or embarrassment before their peers, customers or clients

Looked at in any light, are all of these things not just considerations and marks of respect that any human being would want to enjoy?

SUMMARY

An organisational culture in which employees are motivated and empowered to give of their very best is no longer a 'nice to have'. In a world where a high salary has long since ceased to be the primary motivator, employers need to be exploring the possibilities of recognising and rewarding their employee's in new and innovative ways if they are to have any hope of attracting and retaining the very best employees.

Not just Generation Y and Millennial workers, but employees of all generations are seeking positions within companies that treat their employees as more than just numbers on pay cheques. The ones that truly appreciate that there is often no clear divide between work and home and their employees can't conveniently bring their 'work selves' to work and leave the rest behind. They seek out the employers who understand what it means to strive for an overall feeling of contentment and fulfilment in life.

Whether it's by giving them a reward for a job well done, looking after the comfort, health and well-being of your workers, repaying them in useful and thoughtful ways for the additional effort they put in when they have to work away from home or acknowledging the part played by their loved ones in making your company a success. These are the types of things that will keep your employee's loyal and motivated to deliver their strongest performance.

If you're still not convinced that the benefits of improving your business culture and environment outweigh the often insignificant costs, let's end with a few facts and figures from a recent article on the costs of unhappy employees in the US that might just change your mind...

With improved work relationships and environment, 58% of employees are more likely to voluntarily help their colleagues and 98% will more strongly identify with the company culture

---

Presenteeism (when a worker is physically present in the workplace but lacks productivity) costs the country approximately $200 billion per year and 60% of workers attribute recurring instances of presenteeism to stress

---

Over half of the 550 million lost working days in the US are due to absenteeism caused by stress. These lost days cost US businesses $30 billion every year

---

83% of employers aren't able to accurately guess the amount of stress or anxiety in the workplace and only 14% of senior managers have a formal mental health policy and feel that it has been effective

---

Maintaining happy employees decreases sick leave by 67% and could cut labour turnover costs by $2.3 billion every year

---

Happy employees stay **TWICE** *as long in their jobs, which means huge savings in recruitment costs*

A happier workplace means:

More time spent focussed on tasks

More time feeling energised

More effective efforts and more satisfaction in those efforts

Greater time efficiency

Fewer sick days

NOTES